CLODAGH'S
Weeknight Kitchen

CLODAGH'S
Weeknight Kitchen

EASY & EXCITING DISHES TO LIVEN UP YOUR RECIPE REPERTOIRE

Clodagh McKenna

Photography by Dora Kazmicrak

Kyle Books

This book is dedicated to my three siblings –
Mairead, Niamh and Jim. For all the laughter,
sing-songs and tears of happiness and sadness
that you can only have with your sisters and
brothers. Love you to Cork and back!

An Hachette UK Company
www.hachette.co.uk

First published in Great Britain in 2020 by
Kyle Books, an imprint of Kyle Cathie Ltd
Carmelite House
50 Victoria Embankment
London EC4Y 0DZ
www.kylebooks.co.uk
www.octopusbooksusa.com

ISBN: 978 0 85783 887 2

Distributed in the US by Hachette Book Group,
1290 Avenue of the Americas,
4th and 5th Floors, New York, NY 10104

Distributed in Canada by
Canadian Manda Group,
664 Annette St., Toronto, Ontario,
Canada M6S 2C8

A Cataloguing in Publication
record for this title is available
from the British Library

Printed and bound in China

10 9 8 7 6 5 4 3 2 1

Publisher: Joanna Copestick
Editor: Vicky Orchard
Editorial assistant: Jenny Dye
Design: Lucy Gowans
Creative director: Clodagh McKenna
Photography: Dora Kazmierak
Food styling: Lizzie Harris and Hanna Miller
Production: Nic Jones and Lucy Carter

Contents

Introduction **6**

1. Quick Fixes **12**

2. One & Done **44**

3. Meat Free **70**

4. Storecupboard Stand-bys **102**

5. Friday Night Gatherings **134**

6. Quick & Easy Desserts **156**

Index **172**

Acknowledgements **176**

Introduction

These recipes are a collection of my favourite go-to dishes that I cook during the week when I don't have a lot of time or energy to pull together a meal, but still want something delicious, nutritious and satisfying. Writing this book during lockdown was the perfect time to really hone these recipes – with all of us going through the same dilemmas of not being able to go to the shop and cooking at home seven days a week. Dinnertime became a wonderful hour to look forward to every day. I started a daily IGTV cookery series on the first day of isolation and over the months tested all these recipes with you guys. After a few weeks, this amazing cooking community developed, and the tips, ideas and inspiration from all the comments and messages have made this book what it is today. Every day after filming, I spent the afternoon in the garden, planning, potting, weeding and harvesting. This gave me (and still does) such a connection to what is in season and a constant boost of inspiration for creating these dishes.

These recipes are all easy and stress free. There are Quick Fixes that can be on the table in less than 30 minutes – perfect for when you've been stuck in the office and need some fast food when you get home, like the soul-lifting Chicken Noodle Soup or Baked Eggs with Ham. One & Done is a variety of one-dish dinners, including roasting tin meals, one-pot stews and casseroles, which mean less washing up, and includes some great batch-cooks like the Bella Bean Casserole or the Spiced Chicken & Chickpea Curry. Then there's vegetarian dishes for meat-free Monday (or any other night of the week) like Harvest Salad with Kale, Apple, Beetroot & Grilled Halloumi and one of my favourite recipes, Roast Pumpkin, Mozzarella & Chilli. Storecupboard Stand-bys are based on storecupboard staples like pasta and canned tomatoes and don't require a long list of ingredients – dishes like Margherita Risotto and, our house favourite, Prawn, Chilli & Lemon Linguine. Friday Night Gatherings are satisfying and substantial weeknight suppers for friends and family – Fish Tacos with Pea Guacamole and Ricotta Meatballs with Polenta. Finally, I've also included some easy desserts like my Quick Rosewater Chocolate Mousses and the Lemon Cheesecake that became one of my hit IGTV episodes! There's also a section on Storecupboard Essentials (page 8), a curated list of ingredients that I know will make cooking so much more enjoyable, and the recipes for three of my most-used sauces – Basil Pesto, Hollandaise Sauce and Pepper Sauce (pages 10–11).

My dream is that this book will transform your weeknight cooking – make it more fun, and make you happier, as you dance away, spinning around the ingredients in your simmering pot!

Love Clo xx

Storecupboard Essentials

WHAT I HAVE IN MY CUPBOARDS

OILS – extra virgin and olive, rapeseed, sunflower, vegetable and coconut

VINEGARS – white wine, sherry, cider, balsamic, red wine

SPICES – cumin, turmeric, coriander, paprika, curry powder, chilli flakes, cinnamon, cardamom, garam masala, fennel seeds, ground ginger, cloves, nutmeg, mustard seeds

NUTS & SEEDS – almonds, hazelnuts, walnuts, pine nuts, sesame seeds, pumpkin seeds, sunflower seeds

FLOURS – plain, wholemeal, chickpea, pasta, gluten-free

SUGARS – caster, granulated, muscovado, brown

RICE – basmati, brown, risotto

PASTA – linguine, penne, spaghetti, tagliatelle

NOODLES – rice, egg, soba

GRAINS – quinoa, bulgur wheat, couscous, polenta, pearl barley

CANS – chickpeas, cannellini/red kidney/aduki beans, cherry tomatoes, coconut milk

JARS – capers, gherkins, preserved lemons, sun-dried tomatoes, Dijon and English mustard, harissa paste, honey, tahini, maple syrup, soy sauce, fish sauce, horseradish

OTHER – stock cubes, porridge oats, cocoa powder, bicarbonate of soda, baking powder, raisins, dried yeast

WHAT I HAVE IN MY FRIDGE

Milk

Butter

Mascarpone

Crème fraîche

Cream

Greek yogurt

Cheese – Parmesan, Cheddar and feta

Pastry – filo, shortcrust, puff

Tofu

Salad leaves

Kale and spinach

Fresh herbs

Olives

Eggs

Bacon

Hummus

Tomato purée

WHAT I HAVE IN MY VEGETABLE BOX

Lemons

Limes

Garlic

Onions – shallots and Spanish

Ginger

Cabbage

Carrots

Leeks

Beetroot

Parsnips

Potatoes – sweet, baking, roasting and boiling

Any seasonal vegetables

WHAT I HAVE IN MY FREEZER

Bread

Peas

Spinach

Mixed soft fruit and berries

Vegetable and chicken stock

Pancetta

Chicken breasts

Minced beef and pork

Crabmeat

Prawns

Fresh pasta

Sauces

Basil Pesto

Makes 900ml (1¾ pints)

500g (1lb 2oz) fresh basil leaves

700ml (1¼ pints) extra virgin olive oil

100g (3½oz) pine nuts, toasted

200g (7oz) Parmesan cheese, grated

2 garlic cloves, crushed

sea salt and freshly ground black pepper

Place all the ingredients in a food processor and season with salt and pepper. Blend until you reach a smooth consistency. Cover with a layer of oil and keep for up to 2 weeks in the the fridge.

Pepper Sauce

Makes 200ml (7fl oz)

185ml (6½fl oz) beef stock

125ml (4fl oz) double cream

3 teaspoons coarsely crushed whole black peppercorns

Place all the ingredients in a saucepan over a medium heat and stir. Once the sauce starts to come to the boil, reduce the heat to low and simmer for 15 minutes. Taste and add more black pepper if you wish.

My Everyday Salad Dressing

Makes 600ml (20fl oz)

100ml (3½fl oz) freshly squeezed lemon juice

100ml (3½fl oz) extra virgin olive oil

3 teaspoons Dijon mustard

3 teaspoons local honey

sea salt and freshly ground black pepper

Place all the ingredients in a bowl and whisk together. Check the taste and adjust the seasoning if necessary. This dressing will keep for up to a month in the fridge.

Hollandaise Sauce

Serves 4

100g (3½oz) salted butter

2 medium free-range egg yolks

juice of ½ lemon

sea salt and freshly ground white pepper

Melt the butter in a saucepan over a medium heat.

While the butter is melting, pour the egg yolks into a food processor, followed by the lemon juice. Turn the food processor on to medium speed and slowly pour the melted butter through the nozzle until all the butter is combined with the egg yolks and the sauce has a thick consistency. Season with salt and white pepper.

Gooey Gruyère Omelette

We have a competition at home for who can make the best omelette! Frying pans are at the ready, ingredients are laid out and the next 10 minutes are heads down (barely talking!) and whizzing together our best efforts – it's so much fun. This variation of the omelette was my big winner, and it is yet to be beaten. Made gooey with the beautiful Gruyère cheese and silky with the cream, this dish is peppered with flavours of Dijon mustard and thyme. You can swap the Gruyère for Gouda, Parmesan, Pecorino or Cheddar.

SERVES 1

3 medium free-range eggs

1 tablespoon single or double cream

1 teaspoon Dijon mustard

1 dessertspoon olive oil

90g (3¼oz) Gruyère cheese, grated

1 teaspoon fresh thyme leaves, finely chopped

sea salt and freshly ground black pepper

Crack the eggs into a bowl and whisk together with the cream and mustard. Season with salt and pepper.

Place a frying pan over a medium heat and warm for 30 seconds, then pour in the olive oil. Swirl the oil around the pan so that the pan is coated in the oil. Pour in the egg mixture and cook for a minute. Then draw the egg mixture from the sides of the pan into the centre, allowing the raw egg to run into the uncovered surface to cook. It will only take 2 minutes to cook the egg mixture.

Sprinkle over 70g (2½oz) of the grated Gruyère and the thyme. Cook for a further minute, then fold the omelette in half and serve with the remaining Gruyère scattered on top. Serve with some steamed purple sprouting broccoli, a green salad or grilled courgettes.

Green Gazpacho

SERVES 6

2 celery sticks, roughly chopped

2 green peppers, cored, deseeded and roughly chopped

2 cucumbers, roughly chopped

1 avocado, roughly chopped

1 slice of sourdough, torn

1 garlic clove, crushed

1 green chilli, chopped, plus extra to serve

1 teaspoon local honey

50g (1¾oz) whole almonds, toasted, plus extra, chopped, to serve

60g (2¼oz) baby spinach

a handful of fresh basil leaves

2 tablespoons sherry vinegar

200ml (7fl oz) olive oil

3 tablespoons coconut yogurt, plus extra to serve

sea salt and freshly ground black pepper

This zippy herby soup is so refreshing and bursting with green goodness. You've probably tasted or made a red gazpacho but you may not have tried a green version. I made it again this summer as we had so many green vegetables to use up from the garden, and I had forgotten just how good it was. There are quite a few ingredients but once you have gathered them all it's simply a case of chopping and whizzing them all together in a food processor.

Put all the ingredients in a food processor with 250ml (9fl oz) cold water and season with salt and pepper. Blend until you reach a smooth consistency. Place in the fridge for an hour to chill. If you don't have the time to leave it to chill in the fridge, then add a handful of ice cubes when you are blending.

Serve in bowls with a swirl of yogurt and a scattering of chopped almonds and chilli.

Crispy Galette with Butternut Squash, Feta & Olives

How beautiful does this galette look? Just in case you are wondering, a galette is a rustic free-form tart, and so much easier to make than a traditional pastry tart. I use shop-bought filo pastry made with butter, which is important as it gives that buttery flavour and great crispy texture. The roast butternut squash brings a delicious caramel flavour which works really well with the sharpness of the feta and earthiness of the olives. I sprinkle fresh thyme leaves on top but you can use rosemary or dried oregano instead. The butternut squash can be swapped with courgettes, tomatoes or asparagus.

SERVES 2-4

400g (14oz) butternut squash, peeled, deseeded and diced

3 tablespoons olive oil, plus extra for greasing and brushing the pastry

8 sheets of filo pastry

50g (1¾oz) feta cheese, crumbled

1 tablespoon fresh thyme leaves

12 black olives, pitted and halved

1 teaspoon runny local honey

sea salt and freshly ground black pepper

Preheat the oven to 180°C/350°F/gas mark 4.

Place the squash in a shallow roasting tin. Drizzle with the olive oil, season with salt and pepper and toss to coat. Roast for 20 minutes.

Overlap the filo pastry sheets on an oiled baking tray lined with greaseproof paper, placing each one on top at a different angle so that all the corners create a star-like shape. Arrange the roasted squash in the centre of the pastry, leaving a 4cm (1½in) border uncovered. Sprinkle with the crumbled feta, thyme and chopped black olives and drizzle over the honey. Fold in the rim of pastry around the galette and brush the pastry with olive oil. Bake for 20 minutes or until the crust is golden.

Leave to cool slightly before serving. Serve warm with a green leaf salad, if you wish.

Egg-fried Rice
with Green Vegetables

SERVES 4

2 tablespoons olive oil

4 spring onions, sliced

5cm (2in) piece of fresh ginger, peeled and grated

2 garlic cloves, crushed

1 red chilli, deseeded and finely chopped

800g (1lb 12oz) green vegetables, a mix of chopped fresh beans, frozen peas, broccoli florets, shredded kale or spinach and chopped asparagus

500g (1lb 2oz) cooked brown rice

8 medium free-range eggs, beaten

2 tablespoons light or dark soy sauce, plus extra to serve

juice of 1 lime, plus wedges to serve

I don't know about you, but I always cook too much rice, so this is my way of using up the leftovers when I just need a quick-fix supper with lots of greens and energizing flavours like the ginger, chilli and garlic. You can add in whatever greens you have, so this is a great recipe for doing a fridge raid. I use brown or wild rice because I love the nutty flavour, but any type will work here.

Place a large frying pan or wok over a medium heat and add the oil. Stir in the spring onions, ginger, garlic and chilli and cook for 2 minutes. Add the green vegetables and cook for a minute, then add the rice and stir-fry for 3 minutes, tossing constantly.

Move the rice and vegetables to one side of the pan, pour in the eggs and leave to set, then very softly scramble by stirring with a spoon. Once the eggs are partly cooked but still runny, use a spatula to combine with the vegetables and rice, and then mix in the soy sauce and lime juice.

Serve with an extra dash of soy sauce and lime wedges to squeeze over.

Sea Bass Ceviche with Lime, Chilli & Capers

SERVES 2

2 fresh, skinless sea bass fillets, weighing about 100g (3½oz)

zest and juice of 2 limes

1 red chilli, deseeded and finely diced

2 teaspoons baby capers, finely chopped

100ml (3½fl oz) extra virgin olive oil

1 tablespoon freshly chopped flat-leaf parsley

sea salt

Ceviche is dish that you will probably have come across on a restaurant menu but may not have made yourself at home, and I get that, it sounds quite tricky, but it's really so simple. There are two ways to make ceviche – thinly sliced like I have done in this recipe or cubed into 2.5cm (1in) pieces. The best fish for ceviche are snapper, sea bass, halibut, fluke, flounder, red snapper, halibut and tuna. I just love the fresh citrus flavours of this recipe, perked up with the fiery chilli and salty capers. I serve this with a green leafy salad dressed in a light lemon vinaigrette, as it refreshes the palate and doesn't overpower the delicate flavours of the ceviche.

Thinly slice the sea bass fillets and divide between two plates, spreading the slices around the plates so that you have one layer of fish.

Drizzle the lime juice over the fish and leave for 4 minutes.

Sprinkle the lime zest, chilli and capers over the fish and drizzle liberally with the extra virgin olive oil. Add sea salt to taste, but not too much as the capers are salty. Scatter over the flat-leaf parsley to serve.

Prawn Cocktail

SERVES 4

1 tablespoon olive oil

100g (3½oz) raw Dublin bay prawns, peeled

½ Cos lettuce

2 spring onions, thinly sliced

1 avocado, sliced

sea salt and freshly ground black pepper

FOR THE COCKTAIL SAUCE

2 tablespoons mayonnaise

2 tablespoons tomato ketchup

1 teaspoon cayenne pepper

juice of ½ lemon

1 tablespoon freshly chopped mint

Sweet, juicy prawns bathed in a piquant sauce and served on a bed of crisp lettuce – you have to admit, this does sound like heaven! Prawn cocktail is one of those retro dishes that got a bad rap in the eighties (like chicken kiev), because of the many poor restaurant variations, but it is so good if you use the right ingredients. You need good-quality juicy, raw prawns (it does make a difference if you cook them yourself) and crisp lettuce – Cos like I am using or Little Gem is also perfect. The salad leaves have a refreshing taste in contrast to the piquant creamy sauce. I know ketchup and mayonnaise mixed together with cayenne pepper and lemon juice doesn't sound sophisticated, but it's delicious and nothing beats a classic Marie Rose sauce in a prawn cocktail.

Place a saucepan over a high heat and add the olive oil. Toss the prawns in the oil for 5 minutes until they have turned pink, then season with salt and pepper. Set aside to cool completely.

Separate the lettuce leaves and mix together with the spring onions.

To make the cocktail sauce, mix all the ingredients together and season with salt and pepper.

To serve, put the lettuce mixture into small bowls or large martini glasses. Top with the avocado, then the cooled prawns and spoon over the cocktail sauce. Finish with a twist of black pepper.

15-Minute Pan-fried Plaice with Lemon & Caper Butter

This dish is one of my favourites, mainly because I love fish and it takes just 15 minutes to make from start to finish – a hero quick-fix supper! You can swap out the plaice for any other kind of fish you want. I serve this with buttered or creamed spinach and mashed potato or rosemary and sea salt roasties. If you're not a fan of capers, you can just leave them out.

SERVES 2

80g (2¾oz) salted butter

2 large or 4 small, skinless flat-fish fillets, such as plaice, turbot or lemon sole

zest and juice of 1 lemon

2 tablespoons finely chopped fresh herbs, such as dill, flat-leaf parsley and fennel

2 teaspoons baby capers, drained and rinsed

sea salt and freshly ground black pepper

Place a frying pan over a medium heat and add the butter. Swirl the pan around so that the melted butter is spread evenly over the base of the pan. Add the fish fillets and season with salt and pepper. Cook for 4 minutes, then carefully turn over the fillets and cook for a further 4 minutes. Two minutes before the fish is cooked, sprinkle over the lemon zest and juice, followed by the herbs and capers.

Slightly tilt the pan to the side, so that the juices gather at the tipped side of the pan. Scoop up the cooking juices with a spoon and pour them back over the fish; repeat a few times.

Serve the fish on two warmed plates and pour over all the juices from the pan.

Potato Cakes with Smoked Salmon

SERVES 2

6 slices of good-quality
smoked salmon

5 tablespoons crème fraîche

½ lemon, cut into wedges,
and a little fresh dill
(optional), to serve

FOR THE POTATO CAKES

600g (1lb 5oz) potatoes,
peeled and roughly chopped

50ml (2fl oz) crème fraîche

1 medium free-range egg
yolk

1 tablespoon horseradish
cream

2 tablespoons chopped
spring onions

2 tablespoons plain flour

30g (1oz) salted butter

sea salt and freshly ground
black pepper

Got some mashed potato that needs using up? This a gorgeous way to create a quick supper or brunch dish using up leftovers that might otherwise get binned. I love to serve these potato cakes with smoked salmon, but they also work well alongside a piece of roast fish. For a veggie version, toss some vegetables in harissa and roast them in the oven, then serve alongside.

First, make the potato cakes. Cook the potatoes in a large saucepan of salted boiling water until tender. Drain and transfer to a bowl, then mash with a potato masher. While the potatoes are still hot, mash in the crème fraîche, egg yolk, horseradish cream and some salt and pepper. Then mix in the spring onions. Add 1 tablespoon of flour to help make the consistency suitable for rolling out and sprinkle the remaining tablespoon of flour over a work surface. Roll the potato mixture out to 5cm (2in) thick using a rolling pin and cut into circles using a 10cm (4in) scone or biscuit cutter.

Melt the butter in a frying pan, then add the potato cakes and fry gently for 2–3 minutes on each side until golden brown.

Serve the potato cakes on warmed plates with the smoked salmon, crème fraîche and a wedge of lemon. Sprinkle some freshly ground black pepper over the smoked salmon and a little fresh dill, if you wish.

Garlic & Chilli Prawn Toasts

SERVES 2

2 tablespoons olive oil

4 garlic cloves, sliced

1 teaspoon chilli flakes

12 raw prawns, peeled, tails left on

zest and juice of 1 lemon

1 tablespoon freshly chopped flat-leaf parsley

4 slices of sourdough bread

good-quality extra virgin olive oil, for drizzling

sea salt and freshly ground black pepper

This is one of my favourite Spanish tapas dishes and it has turned into a regular speedy supper in our house as I always have frozen prawns in the freezer. You can add a splash of white wine or dry sherry for extra flavour. I use chilli flakes as I always have them in my cupboard but you can use a chopped fresh chilli too.

Place a frying pan over a medium heat and pour in the olive oil. Stir in the garlic and chilli flakes and cook for a minute, then tip in the prawns. Season with salt and pepper, toss and cook for a couple of minutes until the prawns turn pink.

Pour the lemon juice over the prawns, then sprinkle over the lemon zest and flat-leaf parsley, and toss.

Toast or griddle the sliced sourdough and place two slices on each serving dish. Drizzle a little good-quality extra virgin olive oil over the toasts and spoon the prawns on top, scooping up all the juices from the pan and drizzling over the prawns.

Salmon Niçoise

SERVES 2

2 salmon fillets, skin on, weighing 100–150g (3½–5½oz) each

2 tablespoons olive oil

2 soft-boiled medium, free-range eggs, shelled

4 new potatoes, scrubbed, cooked and halved

12 cooked French beans

125g (4½oz) salad leaves, such as rocket, mizuno, oakleaf or rosso lettuce

2 tomatoes, quartered or 2 handfuls of red and yellow cherry tomatoes, halved

12 black or green olives, pitted

sea salt and freshly ground black pepper

2 lemon wedges, to serve

FOR THE DRESSING

80ml (2¾fl oz) extra virgin olive oil

2 tablespoons freshly squeezed lemon juice

1 teaspoon Dijon mustard

When I was thirteen, I spent my summer in a small village called Châteaubourg, just outside of Rennes in Northern France. My host, Madame Ronsin was a fantastic cook and this is a variation of one of the suppers she used to make for us. It was the first time that I had ever tasted fresh salmon in a salad. She cooked it to perfection – deliciously crispy on the outside and pink and juicy in the middle. The trick with fresh salmon is to sear it on a hot griddle or in a frying pan for just 4 minutes on each side so that it doesn't get dry and overcooked. You can also use fresh tuna instead of the salmon, cooked for just 1 minute on each side. When you are making the dressing, double or triple the quantity and store it in a jam jar or airtight container in the fridge, as it will keep for a few weeks.

Season the salmon fillets with salt and pepper and place a frying pan over a high heat. Pour the oil into the pan and leave to heat, then add the salmon fillets, skin-side down, and cook for 4 minutes on each side or until completely cooked.

Meanwhile, cut the eggs in half and place in a mixing bowl with the potatoes, French beans, salad leaves, tomatoes and olives.

To make the dressing, whisk all the ingredients together in a small bowl or jar.

Pour the dressing over the salad ingredients and gently toss. Divide the salad between two plates, top each with a salmon fillet and serve with a wedge of lemon.

Slow-cooked Squid with Olives, Tomatoes & Garlic

I first had this dish when I lived in Turin, Italy. A wonderful photographer and friend made it for me one day after a shoot. It is a variation on his mother's recipe. Squid should be either cooked very fast (fried) or slowly, like this one, for 30 minutes. The flavour of the squid infused with oregano, chilli, garlic and white wine is sensational! It may take 30 minutes to cook, but it's quick to prepare. You can swap the squid for prawns and if you have any fresh basil definitely add that in too.

SERVES 2

3 tablespoons olive oil

1 onion, diced

2 garlic cloves, crushed

400g (14oz) can cherry tomatoes

200ml (7fl oz) dry white wine

10 black olives, pitted

1 teaspoon dried oregano

1 teaspoon chilli flakes

750g (1lb 10oz) squid, cut into 2.5cm (1in) rings

sea salt and freshly ground black pepper

Place a saucepan or ovenproof casserole dish over a medium heat for 30 seconds. Add the oil, then stir in the onion and garlic, cover and cook for a minute. Next, stir in the tomatoes, white wine, olives, dried oregano and chilli flakes and cook for 5 minutes.

Add the squid rings, reduce the heat to low and cook for 30 minutes until the sauce has thickened. Add a splash of water if the sauce needs to be loosened or if it looks dry. Season with salt and pepper. Serve with some bread alongside for dipping.

Ginger & Preserved Lemon
Crab Spaghetti

This looks like it could be a complicated dish to make, but it's actually one of the easiest to pull together for a midweek meal. It's also sophisticated enough to be a supper party main course. I absolutely love preserved lemons, and they are a must for your storecupboard as they add so much flavour to so many dishes. The delicate citrus of the preserved lemons with the sweetness of the crab, peppered with flat-leaf parsley and heated up with chilli flakes (another storecupboard must-have), all wrapped up in the creamy crème fraîche is delicious. You can swap the crab for prawns or scallops if you prefer.

SERVES 4

500g (1lb 2oz) spaghetti or linguine

1 tablespoon olive oil

3 garlic cloves, crushed

1 tablespoon fresh ginger, peeled and grated

2 teaspoons chilli flakes

1 preserved lemon, diced

300g (10½oz) cooked white crabmeat, flaked

50ml (2fl oz) crème fraîche

zest and juice of 1 lemon

1 tablespoon freshly chopped flat-leaf parsley

sea salt and freshly ground black pepper

Place the pasta in a large saucepan of salted boiling water. Stir for a minute, then cook according to the packet instructions until the pasta is al dente.

Meanwhile, place a frying pan over a medium heat and pour in the oil. Stir in the garlic, ginger and chilli flakes and simmer for a minute, then mix in the preserved lemon. Add the crabmeat followed by the crème fraîche, season with salt and pepper and cook for 2 minutes.

Drain the pasta and stir into the crab mixture. Add the lemon zest and juice and stir together. Transfer to a warmed serving dish and sprinkle over the parsley before serving.

Clam Linguine

SERVES 4

2 tablespoons olive oil

3 garlic cloves, crushed

1 red chilli, deseeded and finely chopped

200ml (7fl oz) dry white wine

800g (1lb 12oz) fresh clams, cleaned

juice of 1 lemon, plus wedges to serve

1 teaspoon dried oregano

600g (1lb 5oz) linguine

2 tablespoons freshly chopped flat-leaf parsley

sea salt and freshly ground black pepper

This dish is known as 'linguine con vongole' in Italy. As the sweet juices of the clams mingle with the white wine, chilli and garlic in this Italian classic, they create a fragrant sauce that coats the pasta – one of my all-time favourite suppers! It takes about 15 minutes to prepare and 10 minutes to cook. The sweet juices from the fresh clams flavour the pasta and broth, so the fresher the clams the better the dish. You can also make this using fresh mussels, prawns or lobster. This recipe is what is known as a 'white' pasta dish, but you can add good-quality canned or fresh chopped tomatoes if you wish; I prefer it without.

Place a heavy-based saucepan over a medium heat and add the olive oil. Stir in the garlic and chilli and cook for 2 minutes. Add the white wine, clams, lemon juice and dried oregano and increase the heat to high. Cover the pan and cook for 8–10 minutes until all the clams have opened. Discard any clams that haven't opened.

Meanwhile, cook the linguine in a large saucepan of salted boiling water according to the packet instructions until al dente. Once the pasta is cooked, drain and set aside, reserving a few tablespoons of the pasta cooking water.

Once the clams have all opened, pour them and the sauce into the drained pasta, add the flat-leaf parsley and toss very well so that the sauce completely coats the pasta. Season with salt and pepper. Use the remaining pasta cooking water to loosen the sauce if necessary. Serve straight away with wedges of lemon.

Chicken Florentine

SERVES 4

4 boneless, skinless chicken breasts

1 tablespoon olive oil

50g (1¾oz) salted butter

300g (10½oz) chestnut mushrooms, sliced

1 onion, finely chopped

4 garlic cloves, crushed

2 tablespoons plain flour

250ml (9fl oz) whole milk

125ml (4fl oz) chicken stock

125g (4½oz) baby spinach

50g (1¾oz) Parmesan cheese, grated

1 tablespoon freshly squeezed lemon juice

sea salt and freshly ground black pepper

Seared crispy chicken with a rich, creamy mushroom, spinach and Parmesan sauce – this is sublime I promise you. It takes about 20–25 minutes to make and it's one of those dishes that will become a regular in your recipe repertoire. If I am really hungry, I serve spaghetti or buttery mashed potato on the side – yes this isn't a dish for 'diet day' but rather one for 'I want something really delicious' day!

Place the chicken breasts in between two sheets of clingfilm. Flatten the fillets by bashing them gently with a wooden rolling pin until they are even in size and about 1cm (½in) thick. Season with salt and pepper.

Place a frying pan over a medium heat and add the olive oil. Add the chicken and sear for 3 minutes on each side until browned. Once browned, transfer the chicken to a plate and set aside.

Return the pan to the heat and add the butter. Stir in the sliced mushrooms, onion and garlic. Season with salt and pepper and cook, stirring occasionally, for 5 minutes. Sprinkle over the flour, stir to evenly coat the vegetables, and cook for a further minute. Pour in the milk and chicken stock and stir until no lumps from the flour remain.

Add the baby spinach and Parmesan and cook for about 30 seconds until the spinach just begins to wilt.

Return the chicken to the pan and simmer gently for about 5 minutes until the sauce is thickened enough so that it coats the back of a spoon and the chicken is cooked through. Stir the lemon juice into the sauce and serve.

Chicken Noodle Soup

SERVES 4

1 tablespoon olive oil

2 garlic cloves, crushed

5cm (2in) piece of fresh ginger, peeled and grated

3 spring onions, thinly sliced

1 lemon grass stalk, thinly sliced

1 green chilli, deseeded and finely chopped

1 celery stick, thinly sliced

500ml (18fl oz) hot, good-quality chicken stock

2 boneless, skinless chicken breasts, cut into 7.5cm (3in) strips

250g (9oz) egg noodles

200g (7oz) pak choi, sliced

1 tablespoon fresh coriander leaves

sea salt and freshly ground black pepper

Warming and nourishing, I call this dish my 'bowl of hugs' as it's so comforting. It's a foolproof recipe that you can make without too much effort when you get home from work. You can add, or swap the pak choi with, lots of other greens, such as kale, spinach, chard or even frozen peas. It is very easy to make your own chicken stock and you will get lots more nutrition from it. And if you have roasted a chicken over the weekend it's a great way to use the carcass. Place the chicken carcass in a saucepan and cover with cold water. Chop a carrot, celery stick and an onion, and add these along with some herbs and any other vegetables that are about to go off, like tomatoes. The only thing that you can't add are starchy vegetables such as parsnips and potatoes. Bring to the boil, then reduce the heat and simmer for at least an hour. Strain through a sieve and you have a delicious homemade chicken stock.

Place a saucepan or casserole over a low-medium heat and add the oil. Stir in the garlic, ginger, spring onions, lemon grass, chilli and celery, cover and simmer for 2 minutes, stirring after a minute. Remove the lid, stir and pour in the hot chicken stock. Stir in the chicken, season with salt and pepper and cook for 10 minutes.

Finally, stir in the noodles and pak choi and cook for 2 minutes, stirring constantly. Ladle the soup into warmed bowls and sprinkle the fresh coriander on top.

Baked Eggs with Ham, Cream, Nutmeg & Thyme

I love baked eggs for supper or brunch any time of the year. They are one of my go-to dinner recipes that I make when I am bit pooped after a long day as they are so fast and easy to prepare. There are so many variations. My favourite is this one, with rich Gouda cheese gently spiced with nutmeg and flavoured with earthy thyme, and then small bites of ham. I serve it with warmed crunchy bread on the side, so that I can scoop into the creamy baked eggs. You can also use pancetta instead of the ham, but just fry it off beforehand. One of my other variations is a tomato-based sauce spiced with harissa, with a crumble of feta and some chopped olives. Smoked salmon with spinach, cream and a sprinkle of lemon zest is also delicious.

SERVES 2

15g (½oz) salted butter

4 medium free-range eggs

75g (2¾oz) cooked ham, shredded

50g (1¾oz) Gouda cheese, grated

1 teaspoon Dijon mustard

¼ teaspoon freshly grated nutmeg

½ teaspoon fresh thyme leaves, plus extra to garnish

2 tablespoons single or double cream

sea salt and freshly ground black pepper

Preheat the oven to 180°C/350°F/gas mark 4.

Grease two small ovenproof dishes with the butter and crack two eggs into each one. Divide the shredded ham between the two dishes.

Place the cheese in a bowl and whisk together with the mustard, nutmeg, thyme and cream. Season with salt and pepper. Scoop the cheese mixture on top of the eggs. Place the dishes on a baking tray and bake for 10 minutes.

Garnish with a few thyme leaves and a twist of black pepper and serve with toasted bread cut into thin slices to dip into the eggs.

Steak Frites & 10-minute Béarnaise

One of my favourite restaurants in Paris, Bistrot Paul Bert, serves one of the best steak frites and Béarnaise that I have ever tasted, and this is my attempt at recreating this French classic. I find baking potatoes are the best for making frites or fries, as they get lovely and crisp on the outside and keep fluffy on the inside. A charred steak, crisp frites and creamy Béarnaise sauce infused with sweet tarragon – absolutely perfect for a midweek supper, or any night of the week to be honest!

SERVES 2

2 sirloin steaks, weighing 300g (10½oz) each

2 baking potatoes, peeled

vegetable oil, for frying

olive oil, for the steaks

sea salt and freshly ground black pepper

FOR THE BÉARNAISE SAUCE

1 small shallot, chopped

100ml (3½fl oz) medium white wine

2 tablespoons white wine vinegar

2 medium free-range egg yolks

125g (4½oz) salted butter, melted

1 tablespoon finely chopped fresh tarragon

Firstly, remove the steaks from the fridge and put on a plate. I like to do this at least 30 minutes before cooking so that the meat comes up to room temperature – it will result in a more tender steak.

To make the frites, slice the potatoes lengthways into 5mm (¼in) thick fries. Place the potatoes in a saucepan of boiling water and cook for 3 minutes. Drain, pat dry and leave to cool.

Place a frying pan over a medium heat and add 5cm (2in) vegetable oil. Once the oil is hot, fry the frites in batches, turning until they are crispy and golden. Transfer to a baking tray lined with kitchen paper and toss in salt.

To make the Béarnaise sauce, place a saucepan over a low heat, add the shallot, wine and vinegar and cook for about 5 minutes until all the liquid has evaporated. Scrape the shallots into a food processor along with the egg yolks. Turn on to a medium speed and slowly pour the melted butter through the feeder tube until all the butter is combined with the egg yolks and you have a thick sauce. Add the fresh tarragon and season with salt and pepper.

To cook the steaks, heat a griddle or frying pan over a high heat until smoking hot. Lightly brush the steaks with a little olive oil and season with salt and pepper. Place the steaks in the hot pan and cook to the following times: BLUE: 1 minute each side; RARE: 1½ minutes each side; MEDIUM RARE: 2 minutes each side; MEDIUM: 2¼ minutes each side; MEDIUM-WELL DONE: 2½–3 minutes each side.

Remove from the pan and leave to rest on a plate or board for about 3 minutes to allow the juices that have been drawn to the surface to relax back into the meat. Serve alongside the frites and the Béarnaise sauce.

Buona Amatriciana

'All'amatriciana' is a classic Italian pasta sauce and became my comfort food when I lived in Italy. It's one of those dishes that makes you feel everything is going to be fine after you've had a hard day, and perfect for when you just want a big bowl of pasta that's popping with sweet, smoky and fiery flavours to make you feel happy. My variation is made with crispy pancetta, but you can easily substitute this with thick-cut bacon or guanciale. If you can't get Pecorino, you can use Parmesan. Use whatever type of pasta you have in your cupboards, but my favourite is spaghetti.

SERVES 4

2 tablespoons extra virgin olive oil

125g (4½oz) thinly sliced pancetta or guanciale

2 onions, finely chopped

1 teaspoon chilli flakes

3 garlic cloves, crushed

400g (14oz) can plum tomatoes

1 tablespoon tomato purée

500g (1lb 2oz) penne, fusilli, spaghetti or linguine

100g (3½oz) Pecorino cheese, finely grated, plus extra to serve

sea salt and freshly ground black pepper

Place a large saucepan or ovenproof casserole dish over a medium heat and pour in the oil. Add the pancetta or guanciale and cook for about 4 minutes until crisp and golden. Stir in the onions, chilli flakes and garlic and cook for 5–6 minutes, stirring often, until soft. Add the tomatoes and tomato purée and season with salt and pepper. Reduce the heat to low and cook for about 20 minutes, stirring occasionally, until the sauce thickens.

Meanwhile, bring a large saucepan of water to the boil. Season with sea salt, add the pasta and cook according to the packet instructions, stirring occasionally, until the pasta is al dente. Drain, reserving 100ml (3½fl oz) of the pasta cooking water.

Add the reserved pasta water and the pasta to the sauce and toss well until the pasta is completely coated with the sauce. Stir in the grated Pecorino and divide between warmed bowls. Serve with an extra sprinkle of Pecorino and a twist of black pepper.

Lamb Chops with Crushed Peas, Mint Jus & Pan-fried Potatoes

SERVES 2

2 lamb loin chops, weighing about 125g (4½oz) each

1 sprig of rosemary, plus extra to garnish (optional)

1 tablespoon olive oil

1 tablespoon finely chopped fresh mint

sea salt and freshly ground black pepper

FOR THE PAN-FRIED POTATOES

250g (9oz) baby potatoes, scrubbed and cut into 1cm (½in) pieces

1 tablespoon salted butter

1 tablespoon olive oil

1 garlic clove, crushed

1 tablespoon rosemary, finely chopped

FOR THE CRUSHED PEAS

250g (9oz) frozen peas

1 tablespoon extra virgin olive oil

1 tablespoon finely chopped fresh mint

I just love a juicy lamb chop! My recipe is a classic, as that's how I like them best. I always have frozen peas in the freezer and a few potatoes lying around, so it makes this whole dish very easy. If you want to jazz it up a bit, you can add crushed fennel to the lamb chops, or cream up your frozen peas by whizzing them with crème fraîche, lime and coriander. A couple of tips for the lamb chops to keep them juicy – remove them from the fridge 30 minutes before cooking and be careful not to overcook them. They should still be pink on the inside.

Remove the lamb chops from the fridge at least 30 minutes before you want to cook them.

Boil the potatoes for 5 minutes, drain and set aside.

Rub the lamb chops with a sprig of rosemary to add a hint of rosemary to the flavour of the meat. Then brush the chops with the olive oil and season with salt and pepper. Place a griddle or frying pan over a medium-high heat and cook the lamb chops for 4 minutes on each side. Keep warm in a low oven.

Meanwhile, place a frying pan over a medium heat, add the butter and olive oil and swirl around the pan until melted. Add the part-cooked potatoes, season with salt and pepper, toss well and cook for 10 minutes, stirring occasionally. Add the garlic and chopped rosemary and continue to cook for a further 5 minutes or until the potatoes are golden around the edges.

To make the crushed peas, fill a pan one-third full with water and bring to the boil. Add the peas and cook for 3 minutes. Drain the peas, then return to the pan and crush lightly with the extra virgin olive oil and mint. Season with salt and pepper.

Divide the crushed peas and pan-fried potatoes between two warmed plates. Place the lamb chops on top of the potatoes, then stir the fresh mint into the leftover jus in the cooking pan and spoon the mint jus over the lamb. Garnish the potatoes with a little extra rosemary, if you wish.

French Onion Soup with Gruyère Toasts

This classic version is made with good-quality beef stock, caramelized onions and topped with oozing Gruyère cheese toasts. Gruyère is the key to getting the bubbling crust because it's rich, smooth and melts easily, but you can also use blue cheese, Comte or aged Cheddar. Sometimes I add a splash of sherry or a cup of stout to the stock – both bring wonderful and very different flavours. It really is the perfect soup supper – rich in flavour, warming and utterly delicious.

SERVES 4

100g (3½oz) salted butter

8 onions, thinly sliced

1 teaspoon dark soft brown sugar

2 garlic cloves, crushed

1 teaspoon dried oregano or freshly chopped thyme or rosemary leaves, plus extra thyme leaves to garnish (optional)

900ml (1¾ pints) good-quality beef stock

sea salt and freshly ground black pepper

FOR THE GRUYÈRE TOASTS

100g (3½oz) Gruyère cheese, grated

4 slices of sourdough bread

Place a heavy-based saucepan or an ovenproof casserole dish over a medium heat and add the butter. Once the butter has melted, reduce the heat to low and stir in the onions. Cover and cook for 10 minutes until soft.

Stir in the brown sugar and garlic and let the onions brown and slightly caramelize, uncovered, stirring every few minutes until they become a deep golden colour. Stir in the dried oregano or fresh thyme or rosemary and season with salt and pepper. Pour in the beef stock and cook for a further 30 minutes.

To make the Gruyère toasts, preheat the grill to high. Sprinkle the cheese over the slices of sourdough bread and pop under the grill to melt.

Serve the onion soup in heated bowls, garnished with a sprinkle of thyme leaves, if you wish, and topped with the Gruyère toasts.

Chickpea Greek Salad
with Herby Lemon Dressing

SERVES 4

8 large vine tomatoes, cut into wedges

1 cucumber, roughly chopped

1 red onion, halved and thinly sliced

16 Kalamata olives

175g (6oz) canned chickpeas, drained and rinsed

150g (5½oz) feta cheese, cut into chunks

2 tablespoons roughly chopped flat-leaf parsley

FOR THE HERBY LEMON DRESSING

zest and juice of 1 lemon

100ml (3½fl oz) extra virgin olive oil

1 teaspoon dried oregano

1 teaspoon local honey

1 teaspoon Dijon mustard

sea salt and freshly ground black pepper

One of my first ever holidays abroad was to the island of Crete, when I was about 14 years old. I remember so vividly this little café that we would go to for lunch every day – it was a small shack perched right beside the beach. That is where I ate my first Greek salad, the fresh, crumbly feta cheese oozing into the sun-ripened tomatoes, earthy olives and crisp cucumber – it was so refreshing and delicious. I ordered it every day of the holiday. I add in chickpeas when I am having it for supper at home to make it more substantial, and pepper it with flat-leaf parsley from the garden.

Start by making the dressing. Place all the ingredients in a bowl, whisk together and set aside.

Place all the ingredients for the salad in a large mixing bowl. Pour the dressing over the salad ingredients, toss together and serve.

Foolproof Three Cheese Soufflés

MAKES 6 INDIVIDUAL
SOUFFLÉS

40g (1½oz) salted butter,
plus extra for greasing

40g (1½oz) plain flour

300ml (10fl oz) whole milk

35g (1¼oz) Parmesan
cheese, grated

80g (2¾oz) Gruyère cheese,
grated

35g (1¼oz) Cheddar cheese,
grated

1 teaspoon Dijon mustard

4 large free-range eggs,
separated

25g (1oz) dried white
breadcrumbs

sea salt and freshly ground
black pepper

For many people, the idea of making cheese soufflés can sound utterly terrifying. I think that's because so much hype has been made about getting that grand lift in the oven, and the fear that it will all flop! But I promise you they couldn't be simpler to make, and once you experience your first soufflé masterpiece exiting the oven you will be thrilled with yourself. There are just a couple of things you need to remember: make sure your egg whites are whisked until they are completely stiff and don't open the oven while they are baking. These soufflés are perfect as a light supper, served with some grilled purple sprouting broccoli on the side with a drizzle of extra virgin olive oil and a sprinkle of chilli flakes. I also love making these soufflés with Gouda or mature Cheddar cheese.

Preheat the oven to 200°C/400°F/gas mark 6 and put the kettle on.

Melt the butter in a saucepan over a medium heat, then stir in the flour. Continue to stir until a paste forms, which is called a roux. Then slowly whisk in the milk, whisking constantly until smooth – this is a béchamel sauce. Whisk in all the grated cheeses and Dijon mustard, and finally the egg yolks. Season with salt and pepper. Once the cheese has melted into the sauce and the consistency is smooth, remove from the heat.

Grease six 200ml (7fl oz) ovenproof dishes with butter and coat with the breadcrumbs.

Whisk the egg whites until stiff and stir a couple of spoonfuls into the cheese sauce to loosen it. Very slowly and gently fold in the remainder with a spatula. Divide the mixture between the prepared dishes.

Make a bain-marie by half-filling a roasting tin with boiling water and putting it into the oven. Place the soufflés in the bain-marie and bake for 12 minutes until well risen and golden. Serve immediately.

Bella Bean Casserole

SERVES 8

2 tablespoons olive oil

2 onions, diced

2 celery sticks, sliced

4 garlic cloves, crushed

2 teaspoons dried oregano

1 teaspoon chilli flakes

1 tablespoon tomato purée

2 x 400g (14oz) cans cherry tomatoes

2 x 400g (14oz) cans chickpeas, drained and rinsed

2 x 400g (14oz) cans cannellini beans, drained and rinsed

24 pitted black olives, sliced

100g (3½oz) baby spinach

a handful of fresh basil leaves, torn

sea salt and freshly ground black pepper

This was the first recipe I made for my IGTV series at the beginning of lockdown – it ticks all the boxes for an easy-to-make, batch-cook, nourishing supper. Most of the ingredients are storecupboard items, it freezes really well, it's cheap and most importantly it's good for you! I like to serve it with half a baked potato or some rice and a sprinkle of feta cheese on top is also delicious.

Place an ovenproof casserole dish or large saucepan over a medium heat and add the olive oil. Stir in the onions, celery and garlic. Reduce the heat to low and cook for 5 minutes. Add the dried oregano, chilli flakes and tomato purée, stir and cook for a further 5 minutes.

Add the tomatoes, chickpeas, cannellini beans and olives along with 300ml (10fl oz) water and season with salt and pepper. Stir, cover and simmer for 45 minutes.

Lastly, stir in the spinach and fresh basil and cook for 5 minutes.

Serve with some Greek yogurt alongside, if you wish.

Spanish Fish Stew

SERVES 4

2 tablespoons olive oil

800g (1lb 12oz) white fish, such as ling, haddock, hake or whiting, cut into 5cm (2in) pieces, skin on or removed depending on your preference

1 onion, finely chopped

3 garlic cloves, crushed

400g (14oz) can cherry tomatoes

2 tablespoons whole almonds, finely chopped

12 green olives, pitted and chopped

a good pinch of saffron threads, soaked in 2 tablespoons warm water

300ml (10fl oz) dry white wine

1 tablespoon finely chopped flat-leaf parsley

1 tablespoon finely chopped fresh dill, plus extra sprigs to garnish

sea salt and freshly ground black pepper

This recipe is bursting with fresh Spanish flavours – sweet tomatoes, earthy olives, nutty almonds and fragrant saffron infusing the fish. It takes about 20 minutes to prepare and only 30 minutes to cook in the oven. If you don't have saffron, you can use 2 teaspoons of smoked paprika or chilli flakes. I like to serve this dish with herbed rice to add freshness to the aromatic flavours of the stew. Use whatever fresh herbs you have, chop them up finely and mix them through cooked rice.

Preheat the oven to 180°C/350°F/gas mark 4.

Place a frying pan over a medium heat and pour in 1 tablespoon of the olive oil. Add the fish, season with salt and pepper and cook for just 30 seconds on each side, then transfer to an ovenproof casserole dish.

Place the frying pan back over a medium heat and add the remaining oil. Stir in the onion and garlic, cover and cook for 2–3 minutes. Remove the lid and stir in the tomatoes. Season and cook for a further 5 minutes, then transfer to the casserole dish.

Stir the almonds into the fish stew along with the olives and the saffron and its soaking water. Add the white wine followed by 250ml (9fl oz) water, cover with the lid and cook in the oven for 30 minutes.

Stir in the chopped fresh herbs and serve with herbed rice, potatoes or a big green salad and lemon wedges. Garnish with extra sprigs of dill and twists of black pepper, if you wish.

Crab Cakes with Fresh Dill Aioli

SERVES 4 (2 CAKES EACH)

800g (1lb 12oz) cooked white crabmeat

4 slices of stale white bread, made into rough breadcrumbs

4 tablespoons good-quality mayonnaise

2 drops of Worcestershire sauce

1 tablespoon finely chopped fresh dill

zest and juice of 1 lemon

2 tablespoons olive oil

sea salt and freshly ground black pepper

FOR THE FRESH DILL AIOLI

3 medium free-range egg yolks

1 teaspoon Dijon mustard

1 garlic clove, crushed

1 tablespoon white wine vinegar

100ml (3½fl oz) vegetable oil

100ml (3½fl oz) extra virgin olive oil

1 tablespoon freshly chopped dill

Growing up on the coast of Ireland, I was very lucky to have fresh crab on my doorstep – for me it's one of the most delicious foods from the sea. These crab cakes are one of my favourite crab suppers. I like to use about a quarter of dark meat in my crab cakes as it adds a lovely sweetness. You can buy vacuum-packed pre-cooked crabmeat, which makes it easier to whip up these crab cakes. I use fresh breadcrumbs to bind my crab cakes together. Even though I am from Ireland, I don't like to add potato as the flavour of crab is so delicate it tends to get lost with the potato. The dill aioli is gorgeous alongside as the silky texture and fresh sweet dill don't overpower the crab but enhance the flavour. I also love making a guacamole or avocado and tomato salsa to go with this supper and serving it with a green leafy salad.

To make the crab cakes, place all the ingredients, except the olive oil, in a bowl and season with salt and pepper. Mix well and form the crab mixture into eight round patties. Place in the fridge to firm up for at least an hour.

To make the fresh dill aioli, place the egg yolks, Dijon mustard, garlic and white wine vinegar in a bowl. Whisk the vegetable and extra virgin olive oils into the mixture slowly. The mixture will gradually thicken to form a thick mayonnaise. Stir in the chopped fresh dill and season with salt and pepper.

Place a frying pan over a medium heat, add the olive oil and leave to heat for a minute. Then cook the crab cakes for 3 minutes. Turn them over and cook for a further 2 minutes until they are golden in colour.

Serve with guacamole or an avocado and tomato salsa and a green leafy salad, if you wish.

Creamy Chorizo & Garlic Mussels

SERVES 2

1kg (2lb 4oz) mussels

2 tablespoons olive oil

2 shallots, chopped

100g (3½oz) cooking chorizo, chopped

3 garlic cloves, crushed

100ml (3½fl oz) single cream

100ml (3½fl oz) dry white wine

2 tablespoons finely chopped flat-leaf parsley

sea salt and freshly ground black pepper

One of my most cherished memories is of my father bringing home a bag of fresh mussels. I sat up on the counter and helped him scrub off the grit and pull off the beards. These shiny mussels were my first encounter with cooking shellfish. Ten minutes later we were all devouring them, dipping pieces of soda bread in the juices to soak up any leftovers.

A simple mussels supper takes no more than 20 minutes and there are so many variations. Swap the cream for canned cherry tomatoes, the chorizo for pancetta or add some samphire. So, what mussels should you buy? Not the frozen, pre-cooked or vacuum-packed ones, that's for sure. Look for rope-grown, farm-raised mussels, which are grown from ropes attached to poles drilled into the floor of the bay or ocean. Along with being the best for the environment, these mussels will give you the freshest flavour, texture and aroma, whether they come in a mesh bag or are stored loose on ice.

Start by prepping the mussels. The shells should be tightly shut and if not, should promptly close if you tap them with your finger. If they do not close, they are not alive and should be discarded. Wild mussels will have a 'beard', which is a clump of fibres they use to navigate and attach themselves to rocks on the seabed. To remove this, give the beard a sharp tug and pull it towards the hinge of the mussel before discarding.

Next, rinse the mussels in cold water to remove any sand and, using a knife, carefully scrape off any barnacles.

Heat the oil in a large saucepan over a medium-low heat. Stir in the shallots and chorizo and cook for 1 minute, add the garlic and cook for a further 2 minutes. Increase the heat to high and stir in the cream and white wine, followed by the mussels. Season with salt and pepper, stir well, cover, and cook for 6–8 minutes. Discard any mussels that haven't opened.

Sprinkle over the flat-leaf parsley and serve alongside some crusty bread for mopping up the juices.

Montauk Seafood Pot

SERVES 4

800g (1lb 12oz) new potatoes, washed and halved

300ml (10fl oz) dry white wine

4 small corn on the cob, about 7.5–10cm (3–4in) long

24 clams, cleaned

12 mussels, cleaned (see page 55)

1 lemon, cut into wedges

16 raw Dublin bay prawns, unpeeled

200g (7oz) salted butter, melted

1 tablespoon flat-leaf parsley, chopped

sea salt and freshly ground black pepper

Montauk is a fishing town and beach spot right at the tip of the Hamptons, about a two hours' drive outside New York. My dear friend Kat McCord has the most beautiful wooden beach house there and so I have been lucky enough to visit a few times. There is such a fun tradition of cooking a clambake on the beach. You simply layer a large saucepan with potatoes, corn husks, fresh lobster, mussels and clams. The pot of seafood is then cooked over a small fire. I wanted to recreate this delicious memory as something we can all do at home, and the result was this fish dish. I have added spicy chorizo, red onion and garlic because I love the spicy flavours they bring to the vegetables and seafood. It's a brilliant one-pot supper and looks fantastic served in the centre of the table so that everyone can help themselves.

In a large stockpot, bring 200ml (7fl oz) water to the boil. Add the potatoes and cook for 8 minutes.

Next add the white wine, corn, clams, mussels and lemon wedges and season with salt and pepper. Cover the pot with a lid and cook over a high heat for 10–12 minutes until the clams have opened. Add the prawns in a single layer, cover, turn off the heat, and leave to sit for about 3 minutes until the prawns are completely opaque.

Using tongs, transfer the shellfish and vegetables to a warmed serving platter or large roasting dish, setting the lemon wedges aside; discard any unopened clams or mussels. Pour the cooking liquor from the pot into a heatproof bowl, jug or small pan and whisk in the butter and flat-leaf parsley. Scrape the flesh from half the lemon wedges into the cooking liquor, discarding the skins and remaining wedges. Pour the butter sauce over the shellfish and vegetables and serve.

Spiced Chicken & Chickpea Curry

SERVES 6

2 tablespoons olive oil

6 bone-in chicken legs
(thigh and drumstick),
skin on

2 large onions, diced

4 garlic cloves, crushed

1½ tablespoons fresh ginger,
peeled and grated

2 teaspoons ground
coriander

2 teaspoons ground cumin

2 teaspoons ground turmeric

¼ teaspoon cayenne pepper

400g (14oz) can chickpeas,
drained and rinsed

470ml (17fl oz) chicken
stock

150g (5½oz) baby spinach

sea salt and freshly ground
black pepper

TO SERVE

60g (2¼oz) Greek yogurt

60g (2¼oz) flat-leaf parsley,
chopped

brown rice (optional)

I love a one-pot supper. The ease of bringing lots of delicious flavours into one dish that simmers away while I soak in the bath is my kind of heaven. It may seem like there are lots of ingredients in this curry but most of them are just spices. And if you have a well-stocked storecupboard then this recipe will be so easy for you to throw together. It's important to seal and brown the chicken first to lock in all the juices and create great texture. The spices also need to be toasted – this brings out their natural oils and with that comes much more flavour. I use chickpeas here, but I also sometimes add cannellini beans, or a can of mixed beans. You could substitute the spinach with kale if you prefer or add in some chopped sweet potato at the same time as the chickpeas. This curry is delicious served on its own but you could also serve it with brown rice, boiled baby potatoes or naan bread.

Preheat the oven to 160°C/325°F/gas mark 3.

Place an ovenproof casserole dish or a large saucepan over a medium heat and warm for 30 seconds. Pour in the olive oil. Season the chicken pieces with salt and pepper. Working in batches, brown the chicken pieces for about 5 minutes until they are golden brown on all sides. Then transfer to a plate.

Add the onions to the casserole, adding more olive oil if necessary. Cook, stirring often, for 3 minutes until the onions are soft and golden brown. Stir in the garlic, ginger and spices, stirring constantly, until the spices are fragrant. Add the chickpeas and the chicken stock. Return the chicken pieces and their juices to the casserole. Bring to a simmer, then cover and transfer to the oven to cook for 45–55 minutes or until the chicken is tender.

Remove the casserole from the oven and place over a low heat, then stir in the spinach which should only take a minute to wilt. Transfer the curry to a large, deep platter, serve with a dollop of Greek yogurt, some flat-leaf parsley and rice, if you wish.

Chicken Tagine

SERVES 6

2 onions, finely diced

6 garlic cloves, crushed

4 sprigs of coriander, finely chopped

4 sprigs of flat-leaf parsley, finely chopped

4 tablespoons olive oil

juice of 1 lemon

2 teaspoons ground ginger

3 teaspoons ground cinnamon

½ teaspoon ground turmeric

6 chicken breasts, bone in and skin on

pinch of saffron threads

200ml (7fl oz) chicken stock

50g (1¾oz) raisins

500g (1lb 2oz) canned chopped tomatoes

80g (2¾oz) blanched almonds, toasted and chopped

200g (7oz) pomegranate seeds

sea salt and freshly ground black pepper

A slow-cooked tagine with lots of warm spices is my idea of a perfect supper. You can swap the chicken for lamb, pork or beef or add in other pulses such as butter beans for a vegetarian version. If you have the time, reduce the heat and slow cook it for a couple of hours, as the meat will get more tender and the flavours will develop further. To make my jewelled couscous to serve alongside, pour 400g (14oz) wholegrain couscous into a bowl and stir in 1 teaspoon of both ground cumin and cinnamon and 100g (3½ oz) raisins. Pour in 600ml (20fl oz) hot chicken or vegetable stock, cover with clingfilm and leave to cook in the steam for 15 minutes. Remove the clingfilm and separate the grains with a fork. Stir in 3 tablespoons of pomegranate seeds and 2 tablespoons of freshly chopped flat-leaf parsley. Season with salt and pepper and mix well. So easy!

Mix half the onion, garlic, coriander and parsley together in a large bowl. Add 2 tablespoons of the olive oil, the lemon juice, 1 teaspoon of the ginger, 1 teaspoon of the cinnamon and the turmeric and season well with salt and pepper. Rub the chicken breasts with the mixture to coat. Cover the bowl with clingfilm and leave to marinade for 2–3 hours in the fridge, or, for best results, overnight.

Preheat the oven to 180°C/350°F/gas mark 4.

Heat 1 tablespoon of the oil in a frying pan. Fry the chicken for 3 minutes on each side until slightly brown. Put the remaining olive oil, onion, garlic and ginger in an ovenproof pot. Stir the mixture and place the chicken on top.

Heat the saffron in a dry pan for a minute, then sprinkle it over the chicken along with some pepper and 2 teaspoons of cinnamon. Add the chicken stock, raisins and chopped tomatoes and scatter over the remaining fresh coriander and parsley. Cover with the lid and cook for about 1 hour in the oven until tender. Check the tagine regularly, making sure that the sauce doesn't dry out, adding a splash of water or more stock if necessary.

To serve, garnish the tagine with the toasted almonds and pomegranate seeds and serve with couscous and a dollop of yogurt, if you wish.

Mustard, Honey & Tarragon Chicken Traybake with Shallots & Parsnips

Mustard, honey and tarragon is the perfect combination for chicken, and once this traybake gets in a hot oven, the butter and flavours from the chicken start to coat the shallots and parsnips. You could swap the shallots and parsnips for any other root vegetables you have, such as carrots, fennel, potatoes, turnips or celeriac. This is a one-and-done hero!

SERVES 4

6 tablespoons salted butter, softened

1 tablespoon Dijon mustard

1 tablespoon local honey

3 tablespoons finely chopped fresh tarragon, plus 3 sprigs

1 whole chicken, weighing about 1.5kg (3lb 5oz)

4 parsnips, peeled and cut into quarters

12 shallots, peeled and left whole

sea salt and freshly ground black pepper

Preheat the oven to 180°C/350°F/gas mark 4.

Place the softened butter in a bowl and stir in the mustard, honey and finely chopped tarragon, season with salt and pepper and mix well. Rub two-thirds of the tarragon and mustard butter all over the chicken and between the skin and breast meat.

Melt the remaining tarragon and mustard butter in a small saucepan over a medium heat. Place the parsnips and shallots in a heatproof bowl, pour over the melted butter and toss to coat.

Arrange the buttered parsnips and shallots in a shallow roasting tray along with the sprigs of tarragon and place the chicken on top. Roast for 1 hour and 20 minutes. Baste the chicken and vegetables halfway through cooking.

Remove from the oven. The chicken will be crispy and golden and the vegetables plump from the cooking juices. Use a piece of foil to tent the chicken to keep it warm and leave to rest for 10 minutes before you slice the chicken and serve alonsgie the roast veg.

Herby Cheese-crusted Chicken Kiev

You may or may not have the most wonderful memories of chicken kiev. It was slightly spoiled in the eighties by the frozen bricks of chicken stuffed with garlic powder that popped up in every supermarket's frozen department. But bear with me. Biting into a cheesy, crispy crumb, then into juicy chicken oozing with fresh herby garlic butter is so delicious, and nothing like the frozen 1980s version. Serve it with a simple green salad or wilted greens such as kale, spinach or chard, or French beans.

SERVES 4

6 garlic cloves, crushed

100g (3½oz) salted butter, softened

3 tablespoons finely chopped mixed fresh herbs, such as flat-leaf parsley, marjoram, sage and thyme

4 skinless chicken breasts

vegetable oil, for frying

70g (2½oz) plain flour

2 medium free-range eggs, beaten

70g (2½oz) fine dried breadcrumbs

100g (3½oz) Cheddar cheese, finely grated

sea salt and freshly ground black pepper

Mix together the garlic, butter and 2 tablespoons of the fresh herbs in a bowl and season with salt and pepper. Spoon the garlic and herb butter on to a piece of clingfilm, roll up into the shape of a sausage and chill in the fridge for 30 minutes or in the freezer for 10 minutes.

Place the chicken breasts between two sheets of clingfilm. Flatten the fillets by bashing them gently with a wooden rolling pin until they are even in size and about 1cm (½in) thick.

Slice the garlic and herb butter into discs that are about 1cm (½in) thick. Divide the discs of butter between the flattened chicken breasts and place on one side of the chicken breast, then fold the non-buttered side on top. Press down the edges of each chicken breast and pinch with your fingers. Cover with clingfilm and chill in the fridge for 30 minutes.

Preheat the oven to 180°C/350°F/gas mark 4. Place an ovenproof frying pan over a medium-high heat and add enough vegetable oil to fill 2cm (¾in) deep. Place the flour on a plate and season with salt and pepper. Pour the beaten eggs on to a shallow plate, then mix together the breadcrumbs, the remaining fresh herbs and the Cheddar cheese on another plate. Remove the chicken from the fridge, dip each breast in the seasoned flour, then the egg and lastly in the cheese and herb breadcrumbs to coat.

Fry each breast in the vegetable oil for 2 minutes on each side or until golden. Then transfer to the oven and cook for 20 minutes until golden and crisp.

I like to serve the chicken kievs sliced on a warmed platter with a dressed green salad alongside.

Spanish Chicken & Rice

SERVES 4

3 tablespoons olive oil

4 chicken breasts, skin on

1 onion, sliced

3 garlic cloves, crushed

10cm (4in) piece of cooking chorizo, chopped

300g (10½oz) paella rice

600ml (20fl oz) chicken stock

juice of 1 lemon

1 tablespoon smoked paprika

24 black olives, pitted and chopped

6 jarred red piquillo peppers, sliced into strips

2 tablespoons finely chopped flat-leaf parsley

sea salt and freshly ground black pepper

This simple one-pot supper is packed with the delicious flavours of chorizo, paprika, garlic and olives to give your taste buds a fresh sensation. It's a sort of chicken paella that you can bring straight from the stove to the table for everyone to help themselves. You can swap the chicken for pork or meaty fish such as monkfish, hake or cod. I like to serve it alongside a big bowl of steamed greens like kale or purple sprouting broccoli, sprinkled with pumpkin and sunflower seeds, or a green leafy salad with a zesty orange dressing. Just whisk together the zest and juice of 1 orange, 200ml (7fl oz) extra virgin olive oil, 1 teaspoon of Dijon mustard, 1 teaspoon of honey and season with salt and pepper, et voilà!

Place a paella pan or an ovenproof casserole dish over a medium heat and add 2 tablespoons of the oil. Once the oil is hot, cook the chicken breasts for 3 minutes on each side until browned, then set aside on a plate.

Add the remaining oil to the pan, stir in the onion, garlic and chorizo and fry gently for 3 minutes. Pour in the rice, stir for a minute, then add the chicken stock, lemon juice, smoked paprika, olives and peppers, and season with salt and pepper. Stir and return the chicken to the pan on top of the rice. Cover and cook over a low-medium heat for 20–25 minutes until the liquid has been absorbed, the rice is tender and the chicken is cooked through.

Garnish with the parsley and serve.

Pineapple Glazed Ham

I love to cook a big ham about once a month as there are so many suppers that you can make from it. Nothing beats the flavour of a freshly roasted ham, especially when it's been glazed with pineapple juice and brown sugar (you can use honey instead if you wish). I love serving it with creamed leeks or colcannon – an Irish mashed potato dish with shredded cabbage folded through it. I use the ham in baked eggs (see page 38), carbonara (instead of the pancetta), in an omelette or with a boiled egg and salad. And let's not forget about the delicious sandwiches you can have from a pineapple-glazed ham – on sourdough bread with a smear of mustard, mayonnaise and some cucumber pickles.

SERVES 10

1 whole ham, weighing about 4.5kg (9lb 14oz), bone in

220g (8oz) can pineapple rings

125g (4½oz) dark soft brown sugar

30 cloves

Preheat the oven to 180°C/350°F/gas mark 4.

Prepare the ham by trimming away any excess fat, leaving about a 5mm (¼in) layer all over. Place the ham, cut-side down, in an ovenproof baking dish, cover with foil and bake for 2½ hours.

Remove the ham from the oven and increase the oven temperature to 200°C/400°F/gas mark 6. Discard the foil and, using a sharp knife, score a 2.5cm (1in)-wide diamond pattern over the entire ham. Drain the pineapple from the can, reserving the juice. Mix together the brown sugar and reserved pineapple juice and pour over the ham. Arrange the pineapple slices on top of the ham, securing them with the cloves. Return the ham to the oven and bake, uncovered, for 30 minutes.

The ham will keep for a week in the fridge.

Aromatic Lamb & Sweet Potato Casserole

SERVES 4

4 tablespoons olive oil

800g (1lb 12oz) lamb shoulder, cut into 5cm (2in) pieces

1 onion, finely diced

4 garlic cloves, crushed

4 sweet potatoes, weighing about 800g (1lb 12oz), peeled and chopped into 5cm (2in) pieces

2 teaspoons ground cumin

½ teaspoon ground turmeric

1 cinnamon stick

400g (14oz) can cherry tomatoes

500ml (18fl oz) hot chicken stock

150g (5½oz) raisins

100g (3½oz) whole almonds, chopped

2 tablespoons finely chopped flat-leaf parsley

sea salt and freshly ground black pepper

This one-pot dinner is packed with the aromatic flavours of Morocco – sweet cinnamon, fragrant turmeric (which also gives great colour and texture), and earthy cumin. The raisins get plumped and filled with the juices of the casserole, but you can also use sultanas, dates or dried apricots. I love to serve this casserole with a cooling raita – yogurt mixed together with fresh mint and grated cucumber.

Preheat the oven to 180°C/350°F/gas mark 4.

Place an ovenproof casserole dish over a medium heat and add 1 tablespoon of olive oil. Tip the lamb pieces into the casserole, season with salt and pepper and cook the lamb for 4–5 minutes until browned. Remove to a plate and set aside.

Return the casserole to the heat, add another tablespoon of olive oil and stir in the onion, garlic and sweet potatoes and season with salt and pepper. Cover and cook for 5 minutes. Remove the lid, stir in the ground cumin, turmeric and cinnamon stick and cook for a further 3 minutes to intensify the flavours. Add the tomatoes, stock, raisins and almonds, stir, then cover and cook in the oven for 1 hour.

Just before you serve, stir in the chopped flat-leaf parsley. Serve with a cooling mint and cucumber raita, if you wish.

Crispy Mustard Breaded Pork Chops with Sweet Potato Wedges

SERVES 4

2 garlic cloves, crushed

1 small shallot, finely chopped

125g (4½oz) fresh breadcrumbs

2 tablespoons Dijon mustard

1 teaspoon fresh thyme leaves

2 medium free-range eggs, beaten

125g (4½oz) plain flour

4 boneless, centre-cut pork loin steaks

2 teaspoons ground cumin

2 tablespoons olive oil

4 sweet potatoes, weighing about 800g (1lb 12oz), peeled and cut into wedges

sea salt and freshly ground black pepper

My favourite way to eat pork chops is like this, breaded with thyme and Dijon mustard and crisped up so that you get that great combination of textures. If you are looking for a sauce to serve with this you must try my Honey and Whiskey Sauce. Put 150g (5½ oz) local honey, 100ml (3½ fl oz) cider vinegar, 100g (3½ oz) dark soft brown sugar, 2 tablespoons of Dijon mustard and 100ml (3½ fl oz) whiskey in a saucepan and whisk together over a medium heat until the mixture begins to boil and thicken. Absolute heaven!

Preheat the oven to 180°C/350°F/gas mark 4.

Place the garlic, shallot, breadcrumbs, Dijon mustard and thyme leaves in a food processor. Season with salt and pepper and blend for 30 seconds. Remove and transfer to a bowl

Place the beaten eggs and flour in two separate bowls (or on two shallow plates). Dip each pork chop first in the flour, followed by the egg, then lay in the mustard breadcrumb mixture and completely coat the pork chop

For the sweet potato wedges, place the cumin and olive oil in a small bowl and mix together using a fork. Pour the cumin oil over the sweet potato wedges in a large bowl, season with salt and pepper and toss to coat.

Place the breaded pork chops in the middle of a baking tray and arrange the sweet potato wedges around the pork. Bake for 25 minutes, removing from the oven a couple of times during cooking to toss the sweet potato wedges. The chops will be golden and crispy and deliciously moist inside.

Coconut, Cauliflower & Chickpea Curry

SERVES 4

2 tablespoons olive oil

1 large onion, finely chopped

3 garlic cloves, crushed

5cm (2in) piece of fresh ginger, peeled and grated

1 teaspoon chilli flakes

2 teaspoons ground cumin

2 teaspoons ground coriander

2 teaspoons ground turmeric

1 cauliflower, cut into florets (weighing about 500g/1lb 2oz prepared weight)

400g (14oz) can chickpeas, drained and rinsed

400g (14oz) can coconut milk

juice of ½ lemon

50g (1¾oz) blanched almonds, chopped

sea salt and freshly ground black pepper

This vegan curry is oozing with wonderful flavours – earthy cumin, coriander and turmeric are lifted by the chilli and fresh ginger. It's a great, easy supper. The sauce makes a versatile base and you can add in your favourite veggies, such as aubergines, courgettes, tomatoes, broad beans and peas. You can also add chicken, fish or meat to this dish, if you wish. I love to serve it with a spoonful of cooling coconut yogurt.

Place a large saucepan or ovenproof casserole dish over a medium heat to warm for 30 seconds, then pour in the oil. Stir in the onion, garlic, ginger and chilli flakes and cook for 5 minutes.

Stir in the spices and cook for a further minute. Add the cauliflower and chickpeas and stir into the spices and onion mix. Pour in the coconut milk and add a splash of water (about 50ml/2fl oz). Season with salt and pepper. Stir, cover, reduce the heat and simmer for 20 minutes until the cauliflower is tender. Add the lemon juice and stir through.

Serve scattered with the chopped almonds and a spoonful of coconut yogurt if you wish, plus some basmati rice alongside.

Cauliflower Cheese Baked Potatoes

This is the ultimate comfort food when you need something warming and hearty. I use Cheddar cheese in this recipe, but you could swap it for Gruyère, Comte or Parmesan. Try adding sautéed leeks, kale or spinach to the filling as well. I love to serve a chard salad with these baked potatoes – I chop up the chard and dress it with olive oil, lemon juice, grated Parmesan and chilli. Delicious!

SERVES 4

4 large baking potatoes, such as russets

1 teaspoon olive oil

1 small head of cauliflower, cut into florets (weighing about 400g/14oz prepared weight)

500ml (18fl oz) whole milk, plus 1 tablespoon for the filling

2 bay leaves

60g (2¼oz) salted butter

200g (7oz) mature Cheddar cheese, grated

sea salt and freshly ground black pepper

Preheat the oven to 180°C/350°F/gas mark 4.

Scrub the potatoes, dry them, and rub the skin of each with the oil and a little salt. Pierce the skin of each in three or four places with the tines of a fork, place on a baking tray and bake for 45 minutes–1 hour, depending on the size of the potatoes.

While the potatoes are baking, put the cauliflower into a saucepan set over a medium heat, then add the milk and bay leaves. Cook until almost boiling, then reduce the heat to low, and simmer for about 20 minutes until tender.

When the potatoes are ready, remove them from the oven, slice them open down the middle and use a spoon to scrape out the flesh into a bowl. Add the butter, the cauliflower and the tablespoon of milk, and mash to combine. Spoon the mixture back into the empty jackets, place on a baking tray and shower with the cheese. Return to the oven for about 15 minutes until the cheese is melted and golden. Finish with a generous twist of black pepper to serve.

Harvest Salad with Kale, Apple, Beetroot & Grilled Halloumi

SERVES 2

1 sweet potato, peeled and cut into chunks

1½ tablespoons olive oil

50g (1¾oz) kale, chopped

100g (3½oz) halloumi, sliced

1 apple, quartered, cored and grated

1 beetroot, cooked, peeled and grated

160g (5¾oz) cooked wild rice

50g (1¾oz) whole almonds, toasted and chopped

sea salt and freshly ground black pepper

FOR THE SALAD DRESSING

2 tablespoons balsamic vinegar

6 tablespoons extra virgin olive oil

½ teaspoon Dijon mustard

I go to New York a lot for work, mainly to cook on NBC's *Today* show. While I am in the city, I spend all my spare time checking out restaurants, cafés and food shops to get inspiration for exciting new recipes. This salad is based on a dish from one of my regular lunch spots called Sweetgreen – they serve hearty salads, warm bowls and soups, made to order and sourced from ethical farmers. Their Harvest Salad is one of my favourites. They serve it with chicken but for a meat-free version halloumi is fantastic. It's packed with goodness and uplifting flavours.

Preheat the oven to 180°C/350°F/gas mark 4.

Put the sweet potato chunks in a roasting tin, toss with ½ tablespoon of the olive oil and season with salt and pepper. Roast for 20 minutes.

While the potato chunks are roasting, steam the kale for 2 minutes, then drain and roughly chop. Set aside.

Place a griddle or frying pan over a medium heat, add the remaining tablespoon of the olive oil and fry the halloumi for 2 minutes on each side.

Make the dressing by mixing all the ingredients together in a small bowl.

Place the apple, beetroot, roast sweet potato chunks, kale and rice in a large serving bowl. Toss with the dressing, season with salt and pepper, top with the grilled halloumi and scatter over the almonds to serve.

Sweet Potato Gnocchi with Sage Butter

SERVES 4

800g (1lb 12oz) sweet potatoes

300g (10½oz) plain flour, plus extra for dusting

1 teaspoon sea salt

1 teaspoon freshly ground black pepper

FOR THE SAGE BUTTER

100g (3½oz) salted butter

2 tablespoons fresh sage, finely chopped

A delicious plate of little cushions of sweet potato tossed in crispy, earthy sage and bubbling salty butter. And they are so easy to make – it's literally mash, stir and shape! I use sweet potatoes in this recipe, but you can swap these for regular potatoes, pumpkin or butternut squash. It's also important to note that I don't boil my gnocchi, as I feel this takes away from the texture.

Cook the sweet potatoes, whole and unpeeled, in very little water for 30 minutes or roast for 30 minutes in the oven. Once cooked, peel and mash them well or put them through a potato ricer.

Mix the flour into the sweet potato mash and season with the salt and pepper. Tip the dough onto a lightly floured surface and knead lightly until combined. Shape the dough into four balls. Dust the surface with more flour if necessary. Using your fingertips, roll each portion of dough into a sausage about 2cm (¾in) in diameter. Cut the dough into 2.5cm (1in) pieces, then roll the gnocchi against the front of a fork to create ridges (this will help hold the sauce once cooked).

To make the sage butter, place a frying pan over a medium heat and melt the butter. Add the sage and cook until it is slightly crispy.

Tip the sweet potato gnocchi into the frying pan, mix them gently in the sage butter and cook for 5 minutes, turning to brown each side.

Serve the gnocchi coated in the sage butter.

Sicilian Aubergine Stew
with Cauliflower & Almond Rice

SERVES 4

4 tablespoons olive oil

2 aubergines, diced

2 shallots, diced

3 large plum tomatoes, diced

50g (1¾oz) baby capers, drained and rinsed

50g (1¾oz) raisins

20 black olives, pitted

2 celery sticks, diced

2 teaspoons dried oregano

1 tablespoon white wine vinegar

1 tablespoon tomato purée

sea salt and freshly ground black pepper

FOR THE CAULIFLOWER & ALMOND RICE

1 medium cauliflower, cut into medium chunks

2 tablespoons olive oil

50g (1¾oz) whole almonds, finely chopped

zest and juice of 1 lemon

2 tablespoons freshly chopped flat-leaf parsley

This stew is also known as caponata and is a simmering pot of summer flavours – tomatoes, aubergines, olives and celery salted with capers. You can make the caponata in a big batch a day ahead. It's also delicious served with pasta or fish. I love it with cauliflower and almond rice, as the rice gets plumped with all the flavours of the stew, creating the most delicious bite.

Start by making the aubergine stew. Pour 3 tablespoons of the oil into a large, heavy-based saucepan or ovenproof casserole dish, place over a medium heat and add the aubergines. Cook for 15 minutes until soft. Add the remaining tablespoon of oil, followed by the shallots and cook for a further 5 minutes. Then stir in the tomatoes and cook slowly, so they break down and turn to a soft mush. Add the capers, raisins, olives, celery, dried oregano, vinegar and tomato purée, season with salt and pepper and cover with a lid. Cook over a low heat for 20 minutes until all the vegetables are soft. Stir gently, occasionally, so they don't break up too much.

Meanwhile, make the cauliflower and almond rice. Place the cauliflower chunks in a food processor and pulse until they are just bigger than couscous. Remove from the processor, wrap in a clean tea towel and twist to squeeze out as much water as possible.

Place a frying pan over a medium heat and add the oil. Stir in the cauliflower rice and chopped almonds and toast for 5 minutes, stirring every minute or so. Season with salt and pepper, stir in the lemon zest and juice and the parsley. Cook for a further 2 minutes.

I like to serve this dish on a large platter and let everyone help themselves. My Mint & Basil Yogurt Dip on page 90 would also be delicious alongside.

Sweet Potato Falafels
with Harissa Dip

SERVES 4/MAKES 12

2 medium sweet potatoes, weighing about 700g (1lb 9oz)

1½ teaspoons ground cumin

2 garlic cloves, crushed

1½ teaspoons ground coriander

2 tablespoons freshly chopped coriander

1 tablespoon freshly squeezed lemon juice

125g (4½oz) chickpea flour

1 tablespoon olive oil

sea salt and freshly ground black pepper

FOR THE HARISSA DIP

1 tablespoon harissa paste

200ml (7fl oz) Greek yogurt

juice of ½ lemon

1 dessertspoon fresh mint, chopped, plus extra sprigs to serve (optional)

A delicious, healthy midweek supper that is pretty simple to make. The sweet potato makes the falafels lovely and moist and the spices and lemon perk up the chickpea flour. These falafels are so good dipped in the spicy harissa yogurt. You can also try wrapping them in a warmed wholemeal pitta. Harissa is one of my storecupboard staples, and I would urge you to get a few jars – it has a slow-burning chilli heat, balanced with a sweet smokiness that adds a real depth of flavour to any dish. You can dollop harissa on eggs or avocado toast, use it to marinade vegetables, or add it to couscous or grilled halloumi.

Preheat the oven to 200°C/400°F/gas mark 6.

Place the sweet potatoes on a baking tray and roast for 45 minutes or until tender. Remove from the oven and leave the sweet potatoes to cool, then peel them.

Put the sweet potatoes, cumin, garlic, ground and fresh coriander, lemon juice and chickpea flour in a large bowl. Season well with salt and pepper and mash until smooth. Shape into 12 small patties and place in the fridge for an hour to firm up.

Place a frying pan over a medium heat and add the oil. When the oil is warm, add the falafels and brown on each side. Reduce the heat and allow to warm through for about 10 minutes.

To make the harissa dip, place all the ingredients in a small bowl and whisk together. Season with salt and pepper to taste.

Serve the sweet potato falafels on warm plates with a dollop of the harissa dip and a sprig of fresh mint, if you wish. Any leftover dip will keep in the fridge for up to a week.

Honey-roasted Carrots with Torn Burrata & Salsa Rustica

Roasting carrots in honey is an absolute must! The sweetness of the honey with the carrots is just so delicious. You can also use butternut squash, pumpkin or courgettes instead of the carrots. If you have the carrot tops (the green leaves from the carrots) chop them up and add them to the salsa. Burrata is a soft cow's milk cheese made in Puglia, Italy. It could be mistaken for fresh mozzarella as they look similar from the outside, but once you tear a burrata open you will see it is filled with soft milk curds and cream.

SERVES 4

16 small carrots

100ml (3½fl oz) olive oil

2 tablespoons freshly chopped flat-leaf parsley

2 tablespoons freshly chopped mint

100g (3½oz) whole almonds, chopped

zest and juice of 1 lemon

2 medium burrata balls

sea salt and freshly ground black pepper

Preheat the oven to 200°C/400°F/gas mark 6.

Put the carrots in a roasting tray, toss with 2 tablespoons of the olive oil and season with salt and pepper. Roast for 25 minutes, shaking the tray occasionally, until the carrots are tender and slightly blackened in places. Leave the carrots to cool slightly, then transfer to a serving platter.

Meanwhile, make the salsa rustica. Combine the chopped herbs, almonds, lemon zest and juice and the remaining olive oil in a bowl and season to taste with salt and pepper.

To serve, use your hands to tear each ball of burrata into large pieces, then set on top of the carrots and spoon the salsa rustica over the top. Finish with a little flaky sea salt and a twist of black pepper.

Kale Caesar Salad

There are so many delicious things that you can add into this classic Caesar – purple sprouting broccoli, roast butternut squash, avocado, sun-blushed tomatoes, grilled halloumi, olives, the list goes on! Double up on the dressing as it will last for a couple of weeks in the fridge, and if you want to perk it up stir in some chilli flakes.

SERVES 4

400g (14oz) kale, tough stems removed, leaves roughly chopped

400g (14oz) Romaine lettuce, leaves separated

100g (3½oz) Parmesan cheese or vegetarian Italian-style hard cheese shavings

2 teaspoons pumpkin seeds

2 teaspoons sunflower seeds

FOR THE DRESSING

1 garlic clove, crushed

½ teaspoon Dijon mustard

1½ tablespoons freshly squeezed lemon juice

125ml (4fl oz) extra virgin olive oil

100g (3½oz) Parmesan cheese or vegetarian Italian-style hard cheese, grated

sea salt and freshly ground black pepper

Place a saucepan of boiling water over a high heat and blanch the kale in the boiling water for 1 minute. Drain and pat dry with kitchen paper.

Next, make the dressing by whisking all the ingredients together in a small bowl or jar.

Place the blanched kale, Romaine lettuce and Parmesan shavings in a bowl. Pour the dressing over the leaves and toss gently. Sprinkle the pumpkin and sunflower seeds on top and serve.

Roast Pumpkin, Mozzarella & Chilli

With sweet pumpkin spiced with chilli and creamy mozzarella, the combinations of textures and flavours in this dish are so wonderful. It couldn't be more simple and easy to make – a great quick-fix supper. You can swap out the pumpkin for any type of squash you like.

SERVES 2

1 small pumpkin, deseeded and cut into 5cm- (2in-) thick wedges

2 tablespoons olive oil

2 x 150g (5½oz) mozzarella balls, drained

1 red chilli, thinly sliced

sea salt and freshly ground black pepper

2 tablespoons extra virigin olive oil and 1 tablespoon balsamic vinegar, to serve

Preheat the oven to 180°C/350°F/gas mark 4.

Place the pumpkin in a baking tray or roasting dish. Brush with the olive oil and season with salt and pepper. Roast for 20 minutes or until browned at the edges.

Divide the cooked pumpkin wedges between two plates. Tear the mozzarella into small pieces and scatter over the pumpkin, followed by the thinly sliced chilli. Season with salt and pepper and drizzle over the extra virgin olive oil and the balsamic vinegar to serve.

Huevos Rancheros

SERVES 4

2 tablespoons olive oil

1 onion, halved and thinly sliced

1 red pepper, cored, deseeded and thinly sliced

4 garlic cloves, crushed

2 teaspoons chilli flakes

2 x 400g (14oz) cans cherry tomatoes

1 tablespoon tomato purée

4 medium free-range eggs

80g (2¾oz) feta cheese

1 tablespoon freshly chopped flat-leaf parsley

sea salt and freshly ground black pepper

4 slices of toasted sourdough bread, to serve

This Mexican recipe is more well known as a brunch dish, but I also love it as a midweek supper. The tomatoes are stewed with the red peppers, garlic, chilli and gooey eggs and topped with peppery flat-leaf parsley and creamy feta cheese. You can also add spinach, chard, kale, grated courgettes and olives. Serve with sourdough toasts for dipping and scooping.

Place a large frying pan over a medium heat and add the oil. Then stir in the onion, red pepper, garlic and chilli flakes. Reduce the heat to low and cook for 5 minutes, stirring every minute or so.

Next, stir in the canned cherry tomatoes and tomato purée. Season with salt and pepper, stir well and cook for a further 5 minutes.

Use a spoon to make four small wells in the tomato sauce, then crack an egg into each well so they poach in the sauce.

Sprinkle over the feta and place a lid on top. Cook for 4–5 minutes, or for a longer or short time depending on how you like your eggs cooked.

Sprinkle the flat-leaf parsley on top, season with some more black pepper, if you wish, and serve with slices of sourdough toast for dipping.

Courgette Fritters with Mint & Basil Yogurt Dip

SERVES 4
(3 FRITTERS EACH)

2 courgettes (approx. 400g/ 14oz), coarsely grated

3 spring onions, thinly sliced

1 tablespoon finely chopped mint

80g (2¾oz) plain flour

1 medium free-range egg, lightly beaten

sunflower oil, for frying

sea salt and freshly ground black pepper

FOR THE MINT & BASIL YOGURT DIP

1 tablespoon finely chopped mint

1 tablespoon fresh basil, torn

100ml (3½fl oz) Greek yogurt

zest and juice of 1 lime

I love these light and refreshing fritters. You could try adding peas into the mix too as they give a lovely sweet bite. If you like your fritters to be very crisp, make sure you squeeze out any liquid − toss the grated courgettes in a teaspoon of salt and place them in a sieve suspended over a bowl for 30 minutes. If you are a fan of garlic, add two cloves of crushed garlic to the dip.

Start by making the courgette fritters. Combine the courgettes, spring onions, fresh mint, flour and beaten egg in a bowl and season with salt and pepper.

Place a frying pan over a medium heat and add a couple of tablespoons of sunflower oil. Leave to heat for 30 seconds, and then spoon in the fritter mixture, one generous tablespoon at a time, using the back of a spoon to smooth out each fritter into a patty shape. Cook for 2 minutes on each side until golden brown and crisp. You may need to do this in a couple of batches.

To make the dip, place all the ingredients in a bowl and season with salt and pepper. Mix together and serve with the courgette fritters.

Mushroom, Leek & Thyme Risotto

SERVES 4

100g (3½oz) salted butter

2 shallots, very finely chopped

2 leeks, thinly sliced

2 garlic cloves, crushed

300g (10½oz) risotto rice, such as carnaroli, baldo or arborio

100ml (3½fl oz) dry white wine

700ml (1¼ pints) hot vegetable stock

60g (2¼oz) dried mixed wild mushrooms, such as porcini, ceps, slippery jack and black trumpet

100ml (3½fl oz) hot water

250g (9oz) chestnut mushrooms, sliced

1 tablespoon finely chopped fresh thyme leaves

2 tablespoons crème fraîche

50g (1¾oz) Parmesan cheese or vegetarian Italian-style hard cheese, grated, plus extra to serve

sea salt and freshly ground black pepper

When making a risotto, it's important that you use a good stock, and that you add it slowly, making sure that each ladle of stock is absorbed before you add the next. The quality of rice is also key, and, in my opinion, the best variety is carnaroli. The second best is baldo, and then the most common, which is still good, is arborio. But, of course, the heroes of this dish are the mushrooms. The wild mushrooms are so pungent that you can mix them with chestnut mushrooms as I have done in this recipe. And if you are lucky enough to get your hands on a fresh truffle, then adding a few shavings on top before you serve the risotto would be incredible.

Place a large saucepan or ovenproof casserole dish over a medium heat and melt half the butter, then add the shallots, leeks and garlic. Cover, reduce the heat and cook for about 2 minutes until the shallots are softened but not browned. Add the rice and stir for a couple of minutes until it is coated with the melted butter. Season with salt and pepper.

Pour in the white wine, stir and allow the alcohol to evaporate – this should take about 3 minutes. Slowly pour in the hot stock, ladle by ladle, stirring constantly until all the stock is absorbed. This should take 15–20 minutes, but taste as you go.

While the rice is cooking, rehydrate the dried wild mushrooms by covering them with the hot water and leaving them to rehydrate for 5 minutes.

Place a frying pan over a high heat and melt the remaining butter. Add the sliced chestnut mushrooms and cook for 3 minutes, tossing occasionally. Add the rehydrated wild mushrooms and pour their soaking liquid into the risotto.

About 5 minutes before the rice is cooked, stir in the cooked mushrooms and thyme. Add the crème fraîche and Parmesan about a minute before you serve the risotto. Serve with an extra sprinkling of Parmesan and some freshly ground black pepper.

Thai Curry Noodles

SERVES 4

400g (14oz) firm tofu

1 tablespoon dark or light
soy sauce

1 tablespoon cornflour

FOR THE CURRY NOODLES

200g (7oz) soba noodles

1 tablespoon coconut oil

200g (7oz) butternut squash,
peeled, deseeded and cut
into 2.5cm (1in) cubes

2 shallots, diced

2 tablespoons minced ginger

4 garlic cloves, crushed

3 tablespoons Thai red
curry paste

240g (8½oz) mixed
vegetables, such as sliced
red pepper, carrots,
courgettes, mushrooms,
broccoli florets, aubergine
chunks and sugar snap peas

400g (14oz) can coconut milk

3 tablespoons dark or light
soy sauce

1 teaspoon ground turmeric

300g (10½oz) baby spinach

2 tablespoons lime juice

1 tablespoon Thai basil leaves

sea salt and freshly ground
black pepper

For this recipe I use soba noodles, a Japanese noodle made from buckwheat flour and water. They give that silky slurpy texture that is so good in curries and soups, but you could use egg noodles instead. A sprinkle of chopped cashews on top would also be delicious.

Start by preparing the tofu. Cut the tofu into small 2.5cm (1in) cubes and toss with the soy sauce and cornflour to coat. Place a frying pan over a medium heat and fry the tofu until golden and crispy. Transfer to a plate and keep warm.

While the tofu is frying, prepare the soba noodles by soaking them in a bowl of warm water for 3 minutes. Drain and set aside.

Then start making the curry. Heat the coconut oil in a large saucepan over a medium heat, stir in the butternut squash, shallots, ginger and garlic and cook for 5 minutes. Add the curry paste and cook for a further minute. Stir in the mixed vegetables, coconut milk, 125ml (4fl oz) water, the soy sauce and turmeric and cook for about 10 minutes, stirring occasionally, until the vegetables are tender.

Finally, add the spinach and soaked noodles and simmer for about 2 minutes until the noodles are tender but still have a chewy bite. Season with salt and pepper and the lime juice. Divide between four bowls and top with the crispy tofu cubes and Thai basil leaves.

Kimchi Cauliflower Fried Rice

This is a super-fast, healthy and delicious weeknight supper. Cauliflower rice is so easy to make – you just whizz it up in a food processor until it resembles grains of couscous. Kimchi is a staple of Korean cuisine – it is cabbage fermented with ginger, garlic and chilli, and you can buy it in most supermarkets. It has a distinctive sour taste, which goes perfectly with the fresh flavours of coriander, kale, the grainy texture of the cauliflower rice and the richness of the fried egg. It will take you about 15 minutes to make this dish.

SERVES 2

1 small cauliflower

2 tablespoons olive oil

2 teaspoons toasted sesame oil

1 small bunch of kale, central ribs removed, leaves sliced into ribbons

2 spring onions, thinly sliced

150g (5½oz) kimchi

2 tablespoons freshly chopped coriander, plus extra leaves to garnish (optional)

3 tablespoons dark or light soy sauce

2 fried eggs and finely chopped red chilli, to serve

Cut the cauliflower into small florets, then pulse in a food processor until the pieces are the size of couscous.

Heat the olive and sesame oils in a large frying pan over a high heat. Add the kale and cauliflower rice and sauté for 3–5 minutes until the kale is wilted and the cauliflower rice is beginning to brown. Mix in the spring onions, kimchi, chopped coriander and soy sauce.

Divide between two warmed plates and serve with a fried egg each on top, a sprinkle of red chilli, and some extra coriander leaves, if you wish.

Vegetable Wonton & Ginger Broth

Every few weeks I crave this dish – the broth feels so healing and the ginger and chilli are so uplifting. I use shop-bought wontons as there are so many good ones readily available. This is my 10-minute go-to midweek supper, and you can add any green vegetables that you have to hand.

SERVES 2

1 tablespoon olive oil

2 spring onions, thinly sliced, plus extra to garnish

6 slices of peeled fresh ginger

1 litre (1¾ pints) vegetable stock

10–14 ready-made vegetarian wontons

a handful of roughly chopped greens, such as baby spinach, pak choi, kale and purple sprouting broccoli

sea salt and freshly ground black pepper

fresh coriander leaves, sesame seeds, finely sliced red chilli and/or chilli flakes, to garnish (optional)

Place a medium saucepan over a low heat and add the oil. Stir in the spring onions and ginger and cook for 2 minutes. Pour in the vegetable stock and increase the heat to medium.

Add the wontons and greens and keep stirring. They should all only take about 3 minutes to cook. Season with salt and pepper.

Divide between two warmed bowls and sprinkle with the garnishes of your choice, if using.

Sunshine Soup

SERVES 4

2 tablespoons olive oil

1 onion, roughly chopped

2 garlic cloves, crushed

1 potato, peeled and roughly chopped

5cm (2in) piece of fresh ginger, peeled and grated

4 carrots, peeled and roughly chopped

1 litre (1¾ pints) hot vegetable stock

sea salt and freshly ground black pepper

FOR THE FLAT-LEAF PARSLEY PESTO

100g (3½oz) flat-leaf parsley

50g (1¾oz) hazelnuts, toasted and roughly chopped, plus extra to serve

50g (1¾oz) Parmesan cheese or vegetarian Italian-style hard cheese, grated

150ml (5fl oz) extra virgin olive oil

This soup is a ray of sunshine in a bowl! The carrots are so sweet and the ginger adds a great zing, and with the peppery flat-leaf parsley pesto, this soup is bursting with flavour and textures. It makes a huge difference if you prepare your own vegetable stock, which is so easy to do – just add a few roughly chopped carrots, onions, leeks, celery and herbs to a large pot of water, bring to the boil and leave to simmer for a couple of hours. Drain, discard the cooked vegetables and you have a delicious homemade stock. It freezes so well, and I also fill an ice-cube tray with the stock. When I am making a gravy from the juices in the pan after a roast, I just pop a couple of the frozen stock cubes into the pan and it adds a delicious flavour. Double or treble the soup recipe – it will keep in the fridge for a week or in the freezer for a couple of months.

Warm the olive oil in a saucepan over a low heat. Stir in the onion, garlic, potato, ginger and carrots and season with salt and pepper. Cover and cook for 10 minutes, stirring occasionally, until the carrots are tender.

Remove the lid and pour in the hot stock, stirring well, then increase the heat and bring to the boil. Reduce the heat and simmer for a further 15 minutes. Leave to cool slightly.

To make the pesto, place all the ingredients in a food processor, season with salt and pepper and blitz for a few seconds. The pesto should be chunky and not too blended.

Pour the cooled soup into a clean food processor and blend until smooth.

To serve, gently reheat the soup and pour into warmed bowls. Garnish with the pesto and a scattering of toasted hazelnuts.

Creamy Polenta with Green Vegetables & Gremolata

SERVES 2

80g (2¾oz) polenta

1 tablespoon olive oil
or salted butter, plus
1 tablespoon oil for cooking

6 purple sprouting
broccoli stems, cut in half
lengthways

6 asparagus spears, halved

100g (3½oz) fresh or frozen
peas (thawed, if using
frozen)

100g (3½oz) mangetout
(purple or green)

150g (5½oz) mushrooms,
such as chestnut, ceps or
porcini, sliced

sea salt and freshly ground
black pepper

FOR THE GREMOLATA

1 tablespoon extra virgin
olive oil

2 tablespoons finely
chopped flat-leaf parsley

2 garlic cloves, crushed

zest of 1 small lemon,
plus 1–2 teaspoons freshly
squeezed juice and extra
zest to garnish

I started really loving polenta when I lived in Italy, as it has the same comforting effect that you get from mashed potatoes. The vibrant gremolata really livens up the dish with its freshness. If the polenta gets too thick, simply whisk in a little water to thin it out. If you have any polenta left over, pour it into a baking dish and let it set in the fridge. The following day, fry it off in butter and enjoy it with a poached egg and harissa.

Pour 600ml (20fl oz) water into a saucepan over a medium heat and season with salt and pepper. Once the water has come to the boil, whisk in the polenta. Reduce the heat, cover and cook for about 25 minutes, stirring every 5 minutes. Once it has cooked, stir in the tablespoon of olive oil or butter.

While the polenta is cooking, make the gremolata. Place all the ingredients in a blender and pulse until you get a thick salsa consistency. Set aside.

Next, cook all the vegetables by placing a large frying pan over a medium heat and adding 1 tablespoon of olive oil. Then add the vegetables, season with salt and pepper and cook for 5 minutes.

Divide the polenta between two warmed bowls, followed by the vegetables and a dollop of the gremolata on top. If the polenta gets too thick, place it back over a low heat and whisk in a little warm water to loosen it up. Garnish with a sprinkling of lemon zest.

Hash Browns
with Dill Fried Eggs & Harissa

SERVES 4

680g (1lb 8oz) potatoes,
peeled and shredded
(thickly grated)

3 tablespoons grated onion

2 medium free-range eggs,
beaten

3 tablespoons plain flour

4 tablespoons vegetable oil

sea salt and freshly ground
black pepper

FOR THE DILL FRIED EGGS
& HARISSA

1 dessertspoon salted butter

4 medium free-range eggs

1 tablespoon harissa paste

1 tablespoon finely chopped
fresh dill

I love the combinations in this dish – crispy hash browns, silky rich eggs and smoky, spicy harissa. It's super simple to make, takes about 20 minutes and the ingredients are ones that most of us will always have in our cupboards. I cook this a lot when I am on my own at home, as it's my TV supper catch-up special. I fry my egg here, but you can poach the egg too.

Preheat the oven to 110°C/225°F/gas mark ¼.

Start by making the hash browns. Dry the shredded potatoes as much as possible using a clean kitchen towel. Then place all the ingredients (except the vegetable oil) in a large bowl. Season with salt and pepper and mix together.

Place a frying pan over a medium heat and add the vegetable oil. Take a quarter of the hash mixture and place in the frying pan, then gently press to form a patty about 5cm (2in) in diameter. Repeat until there are four patties in the pan. Cook for about 8 minutes on each side until deep golden brown. Remove from the frying pan to a baking tray lined with kitchen paper and transfer to the oven to keep warm.

Wipe the frying pan clean to cook the eggs and place back over a medium heat and add the butter. Once the butter has melted, fry the eggs, then season with salt and pepper.

Remove the hash browns from the oven and serve each one with a fried egg on top, a generous drizzle of harissa and a sprinkle of dill.

Mexican Bean Salad

SERVES 8

400g (14oz) can black
beans, drained and rinsed

400g (14oz) can kidney
beans, drained and rinsed

400g (14oz) can cannellini
beans, drained and rinsed

2 red peppers, cored,
deseeded and diced

300g (10½oz) frozen
sweetcorn kernels, thawed

1 red onion, diced

FOR THE LIME DRESSING

150ml (5fl oz) olive oil

100ml (3½fl oz) red wine
vinegar

zest and juice of 4 limes

2 teaspoons chilli flakes

3 tablespoons freshly
chopped coriander or
flat-leaf parsley

sea salt and freshly ground
black pepper

This is such a fun salad, full of protein and bursting with fresh, spicy and zingy flavours. Try it with mango, avocado or cubes of grilled halloumi, or I sometimes add in shredded Iceberg lettuce for extra height.

Start by making the lime dressing. Place all the ingredients in a small bowl, season with salt and pepper and whisk together.

Add the beans, red peppers, sweetcorn and red onion to a large mixing bowl. Pour over the dressing, season to taste with salt and pepper and mix well. Serve cold.

Sunshine Salad

SERVES 6

5 carrots, peeled and grated

1 courgette, grated

80g (2¾oz) raisins

2 celery sticks, sliced

1 tablespoon freshly chopped mint leaves

50g (1¾oz) whole almonds, toasted and chopped

FOR THE DRESSING

100ml (3½fl oz) extra virgin olive oil

juice of 1 lemon

1 teaspoon Dijon mustard

2 teaspoons local runny honey

sea salt and freshly ground black pepper

This was one of the most popular recipe videos on my IGTV, so I felt that I had to share the recipe in this book. It is pure sunshine to look at and it also feels like you are giving yourself a big dose of vitamin C when you eat it. You can bulk the salad up by adding any pulse, rice or crumbly cheese.

Place the grated carrots and courgette in a large mixing bowl.

Next, make the dressing by placing all the ingredients in a clean jam jar, season with salt and pepper and whisk them together.

Pour the dressing over the raisins and leave them to marinate for 5 minutes.

Add the celery, mint, almonds, raisins and dressing to the bowl with the carrots and courgette. Season to taste with salt and pepper. Toss well and serve.

Four Ways with Baked Sweet Potatoes & Hummus

SERVES 4

Baked sweet potatoes are so good for us, so I love coming up with delicious ways to serve them. They take basically no work to prepare and if don't have much time to cook then just buy a good-quality hummus. I am sure you will love one or two of these ways to enjoy them.

4 sweet potatoes

1 tablespoon rapeseed oil

sea salt and freshly ground black pepper

FOR THE HUMMUS

50ml (2fl oz) extra virgin olive oil

2 garlic cloves, peeled

500g (1lb 2oz) canned chickpeas, drained and rinsed

zest and juice of 1 lemon

60g (2¼oz) whole almonds

2 teaspoons smoked paprika

sea salt and freshly ground black pepper

Preheat the oven to 200°C/400°F/gas mark 6.

Clean the sweet potatoes, place them on a baking tray and bake for 30 minutes. Remove the potatoes from the oven and brush the outer skins with the rapeseed oil, so that they crisp. Return the potatoes to the oven for a further 10 minutes until the skins are crispy.

While the potatoes are cooking, make the hummus. Place all the ingredients in a food processor and whizz until well blended. If needed, add a small drop of cold water to get a smooth consistency.

Remove the baked sweet potatoes from the oven, cut them in half lengthways and spoon the hummus on top followed by your chosen toppings. Season with a generous twist of black pepper, if you like, then serve.

FOUR TOPPINGS

• A small dollop of Greek yogurt and harissa paste

• Basil Pesto (page 10) and chopped whole almonds

• Crumbled feta and chopped black olives

• Crispy cooked pancetta and chopped avocado

Bulgur Tabbouleh with Grilled Vegetables

SERVES 2 as a main or
SERVES 4 as a side

125g (4½oz) fine bulgur wheat

5 tablespoons olive oil, plus extra for cooking

juice of 1 lemon

½ aubergine, thinly sliced lengthways

½ courgette, thinly sliced lengthways

1 large tomato, diced

80g (2¾oz) cucumber, diced

1 preserved lemon, diced

1 tablespoon finely chopped flat-leaf parsley

1 tablespoon finely chopped fresh dill

sea salt and freshly ground black pepper

Tabbouleh is a traditional Middle Eastern dish that usually consists of bulgur wheat, tomatoes, cucumber and parsley. I love adding in lots of grilled seasonal vegetables, depending on what I have growing in my vegetable garden. The smoky aubergine is so good in this hearty salad. You can also add peas, spinach, asparagus, butternut squash or carrots – really any vegetable you want. You can prepare the bulgur ahead of time and I love using up the leftovers in a pitta bread with crumbled feta the next day for lunch.

Place the bulgur wheat in a bowl, cover with boiling water and set aside for 10 minutes. Drain well, return to the bowl and mix with the olive oil and lemon juice. Cover and leave for 15 minutes to soften.

While the bulgur wheat is softening, cook the vegetables. Place a griddle pan (or frying pan) over a medium heat and lightly brush it with olive oil. Lightly brush the aubergine and courgette strips with olive oil, place on the heated griddle pan and cook on each side until they are nicely charred. Transfer the grilled vegetables to a chopping board and roughly chop.

In a large serving bowl, mix together the cooked bulgur, grilled vegetables, tomato, cucumber, preserved lemon, parsley and dill. Season with salt and pepper. Mix well and serve.

Creamed Mushrooms on Toast

SERVES 4

40g (1½oz) salted butter

1 tablespoon olive oil

500g (1lb 2oz) mixed wild or field mushrooms, sliced

2 shallots, diced

2 garlic cloves, crushed

140ml (4½fl oz) double cream

zest and juice of 1 lemon

1 tablespoon finely chopped fresh tarragon

4 slices of sourdough bread, toasted

sea salt and freshly ground black pepper

I absolutely adore this simple supper during the autumn and winter when mushrooms are at their tastiest. The nutty mushrooms swimming in cream with the pungent flavours of tarragon and garlic are utterly delicious. I like to add an extra twist of freshly ground black pepper at the end, and you can also serve a poached egg on the side if you like.

Place a frying pan over a medium heat and add the butter and olive oil. Once the butter has melted, stir in the sliced mushrooms. Toss and cook for 5 minutes, then add the shallots and garlic and continue to cook for a further 2 minutes. Stir in the cream, lemon zest and juice and fresh tarragon. Season with salt and pepper and cook for a further 2 minutes.

Spoon the creamed mushrooms over the hot toast, garnish with a twist of black pepper and serve.

Roast Butternut Squash Carbonara

I lived in Turin for three years, on a square which had a huge outdoor market that started at 7am, six days a week. The stalls were filled with the most incredible produce, from farmhouse cheeses to local seasonal vegetables. It was a chef's dream. I learned so much about Italian cooking, including how to make the perfect carbonara. I add cream and crème fraîche (you could just add one of the two), and I know traditionally you shouldn't, but I love the creaminess they bring.

SERVES 4

1 tablespoon olive oil

175g (6oz) pancetta

1 tablespoon finely chopped fresh sage

700g (1lb 9oz) butternut squash, peeled, deseeded and diced into 1.5cm (⅝in) cubes

3 garlic cloves, crushed

400ml (14fl oz) hot chicken stock

pinch of ground nutmeg

500g (1lb 2oz) linguine

50ml (2fl oz) double cream (or single cream for a lighter option)

1 tablespoon crème fraîche

80g (2¾oz) Parmesan cheese, grated

sea salt and freshly ground black pepper

Place a frying pan over a medium heat and add the olive oil. Stir in the pancetta and cook until browned and crisp, then add the sage and toss to coat in the drippings. Transfer the pancetta and sage from the pan onto a plate lined with kitchen paper and set aside, leaving about 2 tablespoons of the rendered pancetta fat in the pan.

Add the butternut squash to the pan, season with salt and pepper and cook, tossing occasionally, for about 8 minutes. Then stir in the garlic and cook, tossing occasionally, for a further 2 minutes. Pour in the stock, sprinkle in the nutmeg and bring to the boil, then reduce the heat and simmer for about 15 minutes until the liquid has reduced by half, stirring occasionally.

Meanwhile, cook the linguine according to the packet instructions in a large pan of salted boiling water until al dente (ideally time it so the pasta finishes cooking at nearly the same time as the sauce is finished in the step below). Drain and reserve 1 cupful of the pasta cooking water.

Leave the squash to cool for a few minutes, then transfer to a blender and add the cream and crème fraîche (with hot liquids your blender should be no more than half full, so if you have a small blender work in two batches). Cover with the lid, then remove the lid's centre insert. While holding a folded kitchen towel over the lid, blend until smooth. (The squash can be also be left whole and stirred together with the cream and crème fraîche.)

In the same pan that you cooked the squash, combine the pasta, puréed squash and one quarter of the reserved pasta water. Cook over a medium heat for about 2 minutes, adding more pasta water to thin as needed, until the sauce coats the pasta. Toss in most of the Parmesan and season. Serve topped with the remaining Parmesan and the fried pancetta and sage.

Spring Green Pearl Barley Risotto

SERVES 2-3

25g (1oz) salted butter
or 1 tablespoon olive oil

1 leek, diced

2 garlic cloves, crushed

½ celery stick, diced

200g (7oz) pearl barley

125ml (4fl oz) dry white wine

1 litre (1¾ pints) hot
vegetable stock

100g (3½oz) asparagus
spears, cut into quarters

150g (5½oz) fresh
or frozen peas

100g (3½oz) spring greens,
such as spinach, pak choi
and/or cabbage, chopped

30g (1oz) Parmesan cheese,
grated, plus extra to serve

1 tablespoon freshly
squeezed lemon juice

1 tablespoon freshly
chopped flat-leaf parsley

sea salt and freshly ground
black pepper

I love making this vegetarian pearl barley risotto in the spring with all the vegetables from my garden. During other seasons just swap out the vegetables for broad beans, sugar snaps and rainbow chard in the summer, or kale and Brussels sprouts in the autumn and winter. Pearl barley risotto is wonderfully light while being highly nutritious, and it is a great alternative to a traditional risotto.

Place an ovenproof casserole dish or heavy-based saucepan over a low heat and add the butter or olive oil. Stir in the leek, garlic and celery, cover and cook for 5 minutes until they have softened.

Remove the lid, stir in the pearl barley and cook for 2 minutes. Pour in the white wine and cook for 5 minutes until the liquid has reduced and the alcohol has evaporated.

Add the vegetable stock, stir to combine, then bring to a simmer and cook for 25 minutes, stirring occasionally, until the pearl barley is tender and most of the liquid has been absorbed.

Stir the asparagus, peas and spring greens into the risotto and cook for 5 minutes until the asparagus is just tender. Add the Parmesan, lemon juice and flat-leaf parsley and season with salt and pepper as required. Spoon the risotto into warmed serving bowls and serve with a scattering of extra Parmesan and black pepper.

Pasta Amore

This is the traditional Italian 'Cacio e Pepe' recipe and I call it my Pasta Amore because I love everything about it. You just need pasta, cheese, butter and black pepper to make it. It is so fast to prepare, you don't need to think about what you are doing (it's that easy) and the result is the most delicious, silky pasta. No variations required, it's perfect as it is!

SERVES 4

500g (1lb 2oz) long pasta, such as linguine, spaghetti or bucatini

3 tablespoons unsalted butter, cubed

1 teaspoon freshly ground black pepper

200g (7oz) Parmesan cheese, finely grated, plus extra to serve

100g (3½oz) Pecorino cheese, finely grated, plus extra to serve

sea salt

Place a large saucepan of water over a high heat and bring to the boil. Season with salt and stir in the pasta. Cook for 10 minutes, stirring occasionally so that the pasta doesn't stick together, until the pasta is completely cooked. Drain, reserving a cupful of the pasta cooking water.

Meanwhile, melt 2 tablespoons of the butter in a large frying pan over a medium heat. Add the the pepper and cook, swirling the pan, for about a minute until toasted.

Add half of the reserved pasta water to the pan and bring to a simmer. Stir in the pasta and remaining butter. Reduce the heat to low and add the grated Parmesan, stirring and tossing with tongs until melted. Remove the pan from heat and add the grated Pecorino, stirring and tossing until the cheese melts and the sauce coats the pasta.

Transfer the pasta to warm bowls and serve topped with an extra grating of cheese.

Margherita Risotto

SERVES 4

2 teaspoons olive oil

3 shallots, very finely chopped

2 garlic cloves, crushed

300g (10½oz) carnaroli risotto rice

100ml (3½fl oz) dry white wine

400g (14oz) can very good-quality chopped or cherry tomatoes

1 tablespoon tomato purée

500ml (18fl oz) hot vegetable or chicken stock

2 fresh buffalo mozzarella, torn into bite-sized pieces

100g (3½oz) Parmesan cheese, grated

10 large fresh basil leaves, torn, plus extra leaves to garnish

This is bascially a margherita pizza but in risotto form, with all the delicious flavours of the much-loved classic combined in a big bowl. The first important step when cooking risotto is to gently toast the rice for a couple of minutes, as this adds a delicious nutty flavour. Next is ladling the stock bit by bit. This allows the rice to absorb the liquid before the next ladle is added, giving your risotto a beautiful silkiness; a risotto should flow like a river. Carnaroli is my favourite rice for cooking risotto, and if you come across a variety called Acquerello, then stock up as it is the best risotto rice in the world! It's aged for 1–7 years, which makes the starch more stable and it absorbs more liquid than any other risotto rice that I have tried. I promise you that it will take your risotto to another level!

Heat the olive oil in a medium saucepan over a medium heat. Add the shallots and garlic, cover and simmer for about 2 minutes until translucent.

Stir in the rice and cook for about a minute. Then pour in the white wine and let the rice absorb almost all of it. Stir in the chopped or cherry tomatoes and tomato purée, let the liquid come to a bubble, then reduce the heat and simmer for a couple of minutes.

Add one-third of the hot stock and stir. When the rice has absorbed the stock, add another ladle, and repeat until all the stock is absorbed. This will take about 15 minutes, and then the rice will be cooked. After 10 minutes, stir in the mozzarella and continue to cook for a further 5 minutes.

Remove from the heat and stir in the Parmesan. Scatter most of the basil over the top and gently stir to combine. Divide the risotto between warm bowls and top with a couple of pretty basil leaves.

Chickpea, Spinach & Butternut Squash Stew

SERVES 6

1 tablespoon vegetable oil

2 red onions, sliced

1 teaspoon ground cumin

1 teaspoon ground coriander

1 teaspoon chilli flakes

1 teaspoon ground cinnamon

1 teaspoon ground turmeric

4 garlic cloves, crushed

7.5cm (3in) piece fresh ginger, peeled and grated

600g (1lb 5oz) butternut squash, peeled, deseeded and cut into 2.5cm (1in) chunks (peeled weight)

2 x 400g (14oz) cans chickpeas, drained and rinsed

400g (14oz) can coconut milk

400g (14oz) can cherry or chopped tomatoes

200g (7oz) baby spinach

sea salt and freshly ground black pepper

This Moroccan-style stew is a super healthy and easy one-pot supper. Everything in this stew is from the storecupboard except for the spinach, which you can swap for chard, peas, green beans or kale. The spices are so warming and the colour is so bright and vibrant. It's a great dish to cook ahead and also perfect for batch cooking.

Place an ovenproof casserole dish over a medium heat and pour in the vegetable oil. Add the red onions, cook for a couple of minutes, then stir in the spices, garlic and ginger. Sweat for about 5 minutes to soften the onions and intensify the spice flavours.

Next, stir in the butternut squash and cook for 5 minutes, stirring every minute to ensure all the spices coat the squash. Add the chickpeas and cook for a couple of minutes. Then pour in the coconut milk and canned cherry or chopped tomatoes and season with salt and pepper. Reduce the heat to low and cook for 40 minutes, stirring occasionally, until golden in colour and the sauce has thickened. If the stew begins to dry out a bit, just add some water.

A couple of minutes before you serve, stir in the baby spinach.

Serve with basmati rice and Greek yogurt with some freshly chopped mint stirred through.

Coconut & Spinach Dal

If you grow your own vegetables, you probably grow spinach and therefore have an abundance of it for a lot of the year! This is one of my favourite dishes to make when I want an easy warming bowl for supper and it is made with storecupboard staples – red lentils, chickpeas and coconut milk, and a few simple spices. If it starts to get a bit dry, add in hot vegetable stock or water.

SERVES 4

1 tablespoon olive oil

1 onion, chopped

2 garlic cloves, crushed

3 tablespoons tikka curry paste

250g (9oz) split red lentils, rinsed and drained

400g (14oz) can coconut milk

400g (14oz) can chickpeas, drained and rinsed

200g (7oz) baby spinach

juice of 1 lemon

sea salt and freshly ground black pepper

Place a saucepan over a medium heat and add the olive oil. Stir in the onion and garlic, reduce the heat to low, cover and cook for 2 minutes.

Next, stir in the curry paste, followed by the lentils, coconut milk and 400ml (14fl oz) water. Bring to the boil, then reduce the heat and simmer for 20 minutes. Stir in the chickpeas and cook for a further 10 minutes.

Lastly, stir in the spinach to wilt, then season with salt and pepper and the lemon juice. Serve with a spoonful of Greek yogurt and some naan bread.

Noodle Soup with Chilli, Ginger & Green Vegetables

SERVES 4

2 litres (3½ pints) hot vegetable stock

5cm (2in) piece of fresh ginger, peeled and sliced

1 red chilli, deseeded and sliced

1 garlic clove, sliced

4 spring onions, sliced

16 French beans, cut into 5cm (2in) pieces

200g (7oz) purple sprouting broccoli stems

100g (3½oz) kale, chopped

300g (10½oz/4 nests) egg noodles

2 tablespoons freshly chopped flat-leaf parsley

sea salt and freshly ground black pepper

This dish takes just 10 minutes and it's so nourishing. There are lots of variations that you can try – swap in soba or wholemeal noodles and any green vegetable will work well. Also try adding some cooked prawns, leftover roast chicken, pork or beef (shredded). If you are looking for a vegan option – fry some tofu and add it in at the last minute.

Place a large saucepan over a medium heat and pour in the vegetable stock. Stir in the ginger, chilli and garlic. Bring to the boil, then reduce the heat and simmer for 5 minutes.

Add all the vegetables to the hot stock and season with salt and pepper. Next, add the egg noodles and cook for a minute, then give them a good stir.

Finally, add the flat-leaf parsley, stir and cook for a further 5 minutes. Serve in warmed bowls.

Spinach, Leek & Feta Filo Tart

SERVES 4

2 tablespoons olive oil

2 leeks, sliced

2 garlic cloves, crushed

200g (7oz) baby spinach or asparagus spears, cut into 5cm (2in) pieces

2 medium free-range eggs

200ml (7fl oz) double cream

80g (2¾oz) Parmesan cheese, grated

100g (3½oz) crumbled feta or ricotta cheese

50g (1¾oz) salted butter, melted

4 sheets of filo pastry

sea salt and freshly ground black pepper

I made this a lot during lockdown to brighten up our midweek suppers. I use shop-bought frozen filo pastry. There are so many great ready-made pastries available in the supermarkets – definitely stock up on them and then you can whip up tarts like this stress-free. The tart is cheesy, flaky and creamy – I love serving it with a dollop of Greek yogurt, or if I want a spicy kick I'll drizzle some harissa on top. You can also add courgettes, chard, kale, peas or asparagus. I use feta, but you could swap that for ricotta or soft goat's cheese instead.

Preheat the oven to 180°C/350°F/gas mark 4.

Place a saucepan over a low heat and add the olive oil, then stir in the leeks and garlic. Cover and cook for 5 minutes. Stir in the spinach or asparagus and cook for a further 3 minutes. Remove from the heat and leave to cool a little.

In a large mixing bowl, whisk the eggs and then pour in the cream and grated Parmesan. Season with salt and pepper and whisk again. Then fold in the cooked leeks and spinach or asparagus, followed by the crumbled feta or ricotta cheese.

Grease a 18cm (7in) tart tin with a little of the melted butter. Brush each sheet of filo pastry with the melted butter and place the filo pastry sheets in the prepared tin, one by one, at different angles so that each corner of each sheet isn't overlapping on the rim. Spoon the tart filling into the centre of the tin and use the back of the spoon to spread the mixture evenly. Bake for 30 minutes until golden.

Serve warm with a green leaf salad.

Prawn Laksa with Rice Noodles

Sometimes there is nothing better than a warming bowl of simple noodle soup. I love it after a long day of working in the vegetable garden when I am cold and need a bit of nourishment. It's ready in just 15 minutes, and so easy to make. The creamy coconut base balances the heat from the chilli and red curry paste. I have added a couple of pak choi to the dish – you just pop them in after you have added the stock and coconut milk. You could also add chard, kale or spinach.

SERVES 2

1 tablespoon olive oil

1 red chilli, deseeded and finely sliced

2½ tablespoons Thai red curry paste

600ml (20fl oz) hot vegetable stock

400g (14oz) can coconut milk

2 teaspoons fish sauce

100g (3½oz) rice noodles

juice of 1 lime, plus wedges to serve

150g (5½oz) raw king prawns, peeled

1 tablespoon roughly chopped coriander, plus leaves to garnish

sea salt and freshly ground black pepper

Place a saucepan over a medium heat and add the olive oil. Stir in the chilli and cook for a minute, then add the Thai red curry paste and cook for a further minute. Whisk in the hot vegetable stock and coconut milk and bring to the boil. Stir in the fish sauce, toss in the noodles and cook for 2 minutes.

Squeeze in the lime juice, add the raw prawns and cook for about 4 minutes. Stir in the chopped coriander and season with salt and pepper.

Serve in bowls with the coriander leaves and the lime wedges on top for squeezing over.

Tuna, Lemon & Caper Pasta

SERVES 4

500g (1lb 2oz) spaghetti or linguine

300g (10½oz) canned tuna (in olive oil)

3 garlic cloves, thinly sliced

2 tablespoons baby capers, drained and rinsed

2 teaspoons chilli flakes

zest and juice of 1 lemon

2 tablespoons extra virgin olive oil

2 tablespoons freshly chopped flat-leaf parsley

sea salt and freshly ground black pepper

Canned tuna with lemon and capers creates a delicious sauce that is so good with pasta. There are so many different types of pasta that you can use — penne, shells or linguine to name just a few. I prefer solid-pack tuna in olive oil for the best flavour and texture. I sometimes add a small handful of unpitted black or green olives and a large, ripe tomato, seeded and diced, for a delicious variation.

Place a large saucepan of salted water over a high heat and bring to the boil. Once the water is boiling, stir in the pasta and cook according to the packet instructions. When the pasta is al dente, drain and return to the pan with 2 tablespoons of reserved pasta cooking water.

Meanwhile, place a frying pan over a medium heat and add the tuna (in its oil), along with the garlic and cook for 5 minutes. Stir in the capers and chilli flakes and cook for a further minute. Remove from the heat and stir in the lemon zest and juice and 1 tablespoon of the extra virgin olive oil. Season with pepper.

Stir the tuna mixture into the spaghetti, along with the remaining tablespoon of extra virgin olive oil and the flat-leaf parsley. Serve alongside a green leafy salad.

Prawn, Chilli & Lemon Linguine

SERVES 4

500g (1lb 2oz) linguine

1 tablespoon olive oil

450g (1lb) large raw prawns, peeled

3 garlic cloves, finely sliced

1 tablespoon fresh ginger, peeled and grated

2 red chillies, deseeded and finely chopped or 2 teaspoons chilli flakes

2 tablespoons freshly chopped flat-leaf parsley leaves

zest and juice of 1 lemon

1 tablespoon extra virgin olive oil

sea salt and freshly ground black pepper

Juicy prawns pan-fried with sizzling chilli, aromatic garlic and zingy ginger wrapped in linguine peppered with flat-leaf parsley. This is one of my favourite easy-to-prepare suppers, which I developed last year for the *Today* show in America. It takes just 15 minutes to prep and is bursting with flavour. When you are draining the cooked pasta, hold back a few tablespoons of the cooking liquid and once the pasta is drained, stir it into the pasta – this will stop the pasta from sticking together. If you want to upgrade this dish, it's amazing with fresh lobster. I sometimes add chopped ripe tomatoes too. I quite like having a big bowl of green leaves afterwards to cleanse the palate, simply dressed with 50ml (2fl oz) extra virgin olive oil, the juice of ½ lemon and a teaspoon of Dijon mustard whisked together.

Place a large saucepan filled with water over a high heat and bring to the boil. Season with salt, stir in the linguine and cook according to the packet instructions until al dente.

While the pasta is cooking, place a large frying pan over a medium heat, pour in the olive oil, then add the prawns and cook, stirring, for 2 minutes. Add the garlic, fresh ginger and chillies or chilli flakes. Cook, stirring, for 3 minutes or until the prawns turn pink and are cooked through.

Drain the pasta and return to the pan. Stir in the prawns, along with the flat-leaf parsley, lemon zest and juice and the extra virgin olive oil. Season with salt and pepper, toss well and serve.

Indian Coconut & Tomato Fish Curry

SERVES 4

1 tablespoon coconut oil

1 onion, finely diced

2 garlic cloves, crushed

1 stalk lemon grass, peeled and finely sliced

2.5cm (1in) piece of fresh ginger, peeled and finely grated

1 teaspoon coriander seeds, freshly ground

1 teaspoon mustard seeds, freshly ground

1 teaspoon cumin seeds, freshly ground

400g (14oz) can cherry tomatoes

200ml (7fl oz) coconut milk

1 teaspoon chilli flakes

600g (1lb 5oz) skinless white fish fillets, such as hake, cod or haddock, cut into 5cm (2in) pieces

200g (7oz) frozen peas

24 green beans, trimmed

a few fresh Thai basil leaves, thinly sliced

sea salt and freshly ground black pepper

jasmine or basmati rice and 2 limes, halved, to serve

The fish simmering away in aromatic spices, creamy coconut milk and sweet tomatoes and Thai basil is sensational. You can also use chicken, prawns, beef or hearty vegetables such as aubergines, courgettes or tofu in this curry. It freezes really well, so I usually double the recipe and freeze half for when I want a day off cooking.

Place a large saucepan or an ovenproof casserole dish over a medium heat and add the coconut oil. Stir in the onion, garlic, lemon grass, ginger, coriander, mustard and cumin seeds and cook for 5 minutes. Add the canned tomatoes, coconut milk and chilli flakes, stir, season with salt and pepper and simmer for 3 minutes.

Stir the fresh fish into the curry, followed by the green vegetables and cook for 5 minutes.

Scatter the fresh Thai basil leaves on top and serve with rice and lime halves.

Garlic Lamb Cutlets with Crushed Rosemary Cannellini Beans

If you haven't tried crushed cannellini beans, then you are in for a treat. They are utterly delicious mashed and cooked with olive oil, garlic and rosemary (you can also use thyme or oregano), but they are also so simple to make and a fantastic stand-by staple. This dish is perfect on its own, but if you are thinking of adding some sides then roast butternut squash, honey-roasted carrots or parsnips, buttered spinach, or steamed broccoli would all be lovely.

SERVES 2

4–6 lamb cutlets, depending on size

4 garlic cloves, sliced

2 tablespoons olive oil

juice of ½ lemon

extra virgin oil, to serve

FOR THE CRUSHED ROSEMARY CANNELLINI BEANS

1 tablespoon olive oil

400g (14oz) can cannellini beans, drained and rinsed

1 tablespoon finely chopped fresh rosemary, plus extra to garnish

sea salt and freshly ground black pepper

Place the lamb cutlets in a bowl, add the garlic and olive oil and season with salt and pepper. Using your hands (clean ones, of course!), rub the garlic, olive oil and seasoning into the lamb. Cover the bowl with clingfilm and transfer to the fridge to marinate for 30 minutes.

Place a griddle or frying pan over a medium-high heat until hot. Then add the lamb cutlets and cook for 4 minutes on each side. Set aside while you prepare the crushed cannellini beans.

For the crushed rosemary cannellini beans, add the olive oil to a saucepan over a low heat. Pour in the cannellini beans and season with salt and pepper. Using a potato masher, gently squash the beans – you want them to be crushed rather than mashed. Stir in the rosemary and heat through. Spoon the beans onto two warmed plates and arrange the lamb cutlets alongside. I usually finish this with a drizzle of my best extra virgin olive oil and an extra sprinkling of finely chopped rosemary.

Butter Chicken Curry

SERVES 4

500g (1lb 2oz) boneless, skinless chicken thighs

2 tablespoons olive oil

1 onion, diced

4 garlic cloves, crushed

1 red chilli, finely chopped

1 tablespoon fresh ginger, peeled and grated

1 teaspoon garam masala

3 tablespoons tomato purée

400ml (14fl oz) hot chicken stock

50g (1¾oz) whole almonds, toasted and chopped

FOR THE MARINADE

juice of 1 lemon

2 teaspoons ground cumin

2 teaspoons paprika

1 teaspoon hot chilli powder

200ml (7fl oz) Greek yogurt

sea salt and freshly ground black pepper

TO SERVE

basmati rice of your choice

naan bread

mango chutney

lime wedges

If I go out for an Indian meal, this is the curry that I order – the creamy, perfectly spiced sauce is so addictive. I also love making this dish with big, juicy prawns. Make sure you add lots of lime juice and a good twist of black pepper at the end. It freezes well, so double the recipe and freeze half for a rainy day.

Start by making the marinade for the chicken. Place all the ingredients in a bowl, whisk together and season with salt and pepper. Chop the chicken into bite-sized pieces and toss with the marinade. Cover with clingfilm and chill in the fridge for 1 hour.

Place a large saucepan or ovenproof casserole dish over a medium heat. Add the olive oil and stir in the onion, garlic, chilli and ginger and cook for 5 minutes. Stir in the garam masala and tomato purée and cook for 2 minutes, then add the hot chicken stock and marinated chicken. Cook for 5 minutes over a medium heat, then reduce the heat to low and continue to cook for 15 minutes until the chicken is cooked and the sauce has thickened.

Sprinkle in the toasted almonds. Serve with rice, naan bread, mango chutney and lime wedges.

FRIDAY NIGHT GATHERINGS 5

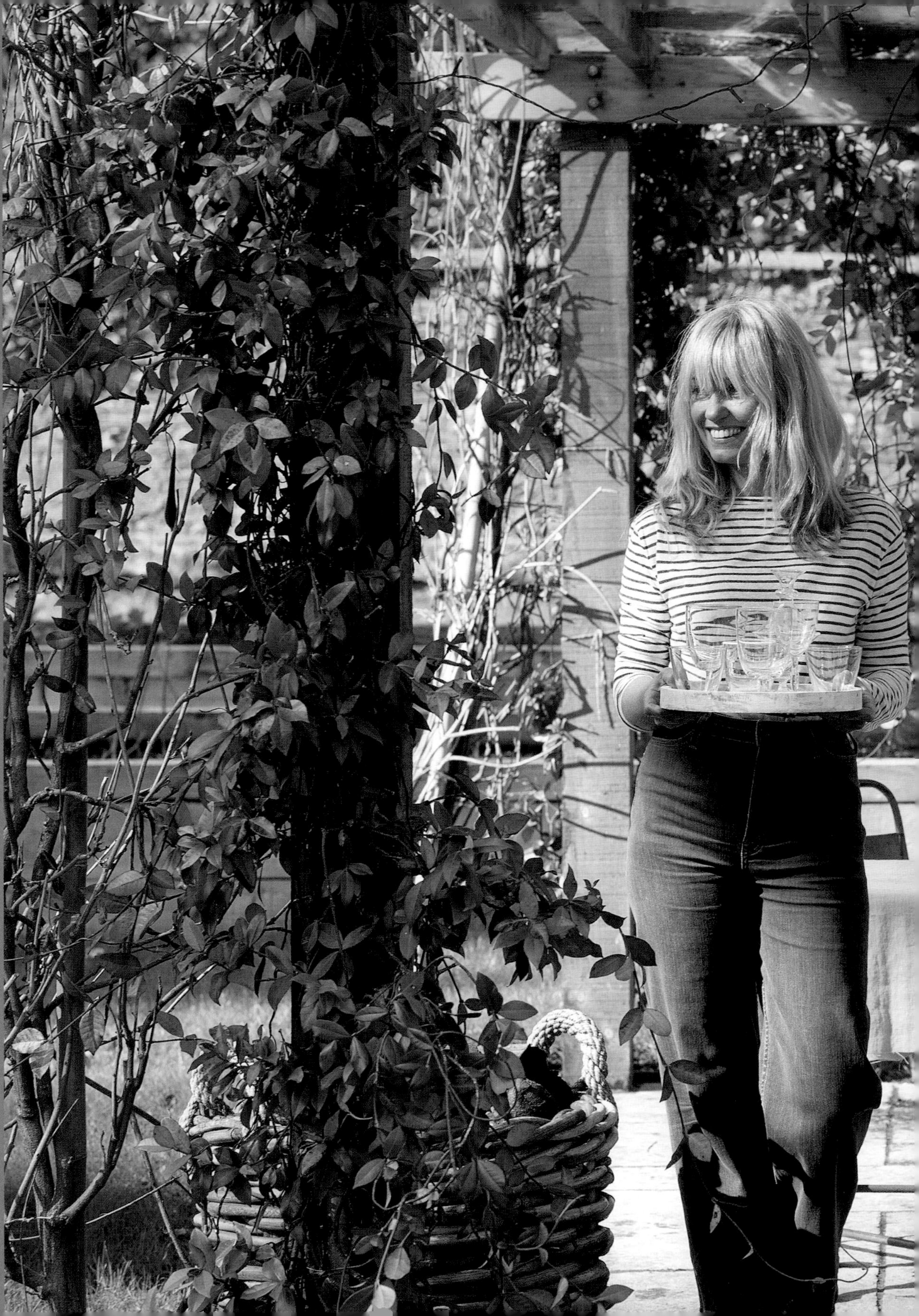

Three-bean Chilli with all the Trimmings

SERVES 6

2 tablespoons olive oil

1 large carrot, peeled and diced

1 large celery stick, diced

1 onion, finely chopped

1 garlic clove, crushed

1 red chilli, finely chopped

1 teaspoon ground cumin

1 teaspoon ground cinnamon

1 teaspoon ground ginger

1 tablespoon tomato purée

2 x 400g (14oz) cans cherry tomatoes

1 bay leaf

400g (14oz) can each red kidney beans, aduki beans and black-eyed beans, drained and rinsed

a handful of freshly chopped coriander or flat-leaf parsley leaves

sea salt and freshly ground black pepper

TO SERVE

Pea Guacamole (page 144)

tortilla chips

soured cream

brown rice

grated Cheddar cheese

This three-bean vegetarian chili is a wonderfully simple, one-pot no-fuss dish. The results are magical, a richly flavoured meal that only gets better with time, like a fine wine, if you can make it a day ahead. Serve it up in a large warmed bowl for everyone to help themselves, along with smaller bowls of guacamole, rice, grated cheese and tortilla chips. The perfect Friday night feast!

Place an ovenproof casserole dish or large saucepan over a medium heat, then add the olive oil. Stir in the carrot, celery, onion, garlic and chilli. Cover with a lid, reduce the heat to low and cook for 10 minutes, stirring occasionally.

Remove the lid and stir in the spices. Cook for 2 minutes, then stir in the tomato purée, canned cherry tomatoes and bay leaf. Season with salt and pepper, stir and cook for 10 minutes.

Next, stir in all the beans, bring to a simmer, cover and cook over a low heat for 15 minutes.

Remove from the heat, stir in the coriander or parsley and serve with as many of the trimmings as you like.

Ricotta, Honey & Thyme Pizza

SERVES 2

6g (⅛oz) fresh yeast

100ml (3½fl oz) warm water

200g (7oz) strong white (bread) flour, plus extra for dusting

100ml (3½fl oz) tepid water

50ml (2fl oz) olive oil, for brushing

250g (9oz) ricotta cheese

1 tablespoon runny local honey

2 teaspoons finely chopped fresh thyme leaves, plus tiny sprigs to garnish

1 dessertspoon pine nuts, toasted

sea salt and freshly ground black pepper

I made this in the oven, but you can also make it in a frying pan. Heat a large ovenproof, non-stick frying pan over a high heat. Reduce the heat to medium and carefully put a circle of dough in the pan. Cook the base for 4 minutes until golden brown. Then brush the pizza base with some olive oil, scatter over your toppings (as in the method below) and finish it off by placing it under a hot grill for 5 minutes or until golden and bubbling. You can swap out the ricotta for soft goat's cheese if you prefer.

Put the fresh yeast into a small bowl, cover with the warm water and blend to form a smooth paste.

Place the flour in a bowl, make a well in the centre and pour the yeast into it. Add a pinch of salt and mix in the flour from the sides. Add the tepid water and mix into a dough. Tip out onto a lightly floured surface and knead the dough by pushing the dough away from you with the heel of your hand until you reach a light consistency. Place the dough back in the bowl, cover with a tea towel and leave in a warm place for about 3 hours to allow the dough to rise.

Preheat the oven to 180°C/350°F/gas mark 4.

When the dough has risen, tip it out onto a floured board and roll out to make a circular pizza shape; I like my pizzas thin, so I roll it to about 5mm (¼in) thick. Then brush the pizza base with some olive oil, crumble the ricotta cheese on top, drizzle the honey over the cheese and sprinkle over the finely chopped thyme. Season with salt and pepper, then transfer to a baking tray or ovenproof frying pan and bake for 20 minutes until the crust is golden and crisp and the cheese has melted.

Scatter over tiny sprigs of thyme and the toasted pine nuts and season with a generous twist of black pepper to serve.

Cheese Soufflé Tart with Walnut-crusted Pastry

SERVES 6

50g (1¾oz) salted butter

50g (1¾oz) plain flour

200ml (7fl oz) whole milk

80g (2¾oz) Gruyère cheese, grated

2 teaspoons Dijon mustard

3 medium free-range eggs, separated, and egg whites whisked until stiff

150ml (5fl oz) double cream

FOR THE PASTRY

80g (2¾oz) shelled walnuts

230g (8oz) plain flour, plus extra for dusting

150g (5½oz) unsalted butter, chilled and cubed

1 medium free-range egg

sea salt and freshly ground black pepper

The light, pillowy cheese filling encased in buttery, crumbly pastry in this tart is incredible. I use walnuts in the pastry as they give a fantastic nutty flavour but you could also use almonds or hazelnuts. The Gruyère could be mixed with Cheddar, and I have also made this using blue cheese, which was delicious. Serve with onion confiture, apple chutney or a tomato relish, and some green vegetables or a salad.

Start by making the pastry. Put the walnuts, flour, butter and a pinch of salt in a food processor and whizz together until you have a breadcrumb consistency. Break the egg into the food processor and add a couple of teaspoons of cold water, then whizz again until the pastry starts coming together, adding a little more water if needed.

Tip the pastry out onto a lightly floured surface, bring the dough together and then shape into a circular piece, wrap in clingfilm and chill in the fridge for 20 minutes.

Preheat the oven to 180°C/350°F/gas mark 4.

Roll out the chilled pastry on a lightly floured surface so that it fits a 23cm (9in) loose-bottomed tart tin. Once you have placed the pastry in the tart tin, lay a sheet of non-stick baking paper over the pastry (like a blanket) and fill it with baking beans or uncooked rice. Bake for 15 minutes.

Remove the paper and beans/rice and bake for a further 10 minutes. Set aside while you make the filling.

Melt the butter in a saucepan over a medium heat, add the flour and stir until you have a pastry-like dough (this is called a roux). Whisk in the milk, whisking continuously until smooth. Then remove from the heat and whisk in the grated Gruyère, mustard, egg yolks and cream. Season with salt and pepper and mix well. Gently fold in the whisked egg whites. Pour the mixture into the pastry case and bake for 30 minutes until the soufflé filling is fluffy and golden.

Serve hot with any of the suggestions above.

Sea Bass & Spring Onion in a Wild Garlic Broth

SERVES 4

4 skinless fillets of sea bass, weighing about 150g (5½oz) each

4 tablespoons olive oil

8 spring onions, trimmed and left whole

2 celery sticks, sliced

4 shallots, diced

3 garlic cloves, crushed

200ml (7fl oz) dry white wine

600ml (20fl oz) fish stock

a bunch of wild garlic, chopped

sea salt and freshly ground black pepper

sorrel leaves and lemon wedges, to garnish

When wild garlic is in season this is one of my favourite ways to cook with it. A delicious broth that brings whispers of garlic to the fish. When I can't get wild garlic, I use a mix of fresh herbs instead – chives, flat-leaf parsley and fennel. Serve with grilled asparagus tossed in extra virgin olive and fresh mint, and buttered potatoes.

Place a griddle or frying pan over a medium heat. Brush the fish fillets with 2 tablespoons of the olive oil and season with salt and pepper. Place the fish in the hot pan and cook for 5 minutes on each side. While the fish is cooking, add the spring onions to the pan and cook for 2 minutes on each side until slightly golden.

Meanwhile, make the broth. Place a saucepan over a medium heat and add the remaining olive oil. Stir in the celery, shallots and garlic and cook for about 3 minutes. Pour in the white wine and simmer for a further 3 minutes. Stir in the fish stock and wild garlic. Reduce the heat to low, season with salt and pepper and simmer for 10 minutes.

To serve, spoon the broth into warmed shallow bowls and divide the cooked spring onions between the bowls. Place the cooked sea bass fillets on top, garnish with sorrel leaves and serve each portion with a lemon wedge on the side.

Fish Pie Baked Potatoes

SERVES 4

4 baking potatoes, scrubbed

125g (4½oz) salted butter

50g (1¾oz) Cheddar cheese, finely grated

300ml (10fl oz) whole milk

1 bay leaf

5 black peppercorns

250g (9oz) fish pie mix, such as salmon, white fish and smoked fish

200g (7oz) raw prawns, peeled

70g (2½oz) plain flour

100ml (3½fl oz) dry white wine (optional)

1 teaspoon Dijon mustard

1 tablespoon finely chopped fresh chives, plus extra to garnish

sea salt and freshly ground black pepper

Fish pie meets baked potato, what's not to love? Created by scooping out the flesh of the potatoes and incorporating it into the pie filling, these are creamy, hearty and so comforting. You can make them a day ahead and they freeze really well. I love serving a large platter of green vegetables alongside – green beans tossed in butter, broad beans with fresh mint, chard with a sprinkle of chilli, or spinach creamed with fresh nutmeg.

Preheat the oven to 200°C/400°F/gas mark 6.

Prick the potatoes all over with a fork and sprinkle with a little salt. Bake for 1 hour or until tender. Remove from the oven and leave them to cool enough so that you can handle them. Leave the oven on.

Scoop out the potato flesh into a bowl, leaving a 1cm (½in) potato shell. Mash the potato flesh with 50g (1¾oz) of the butter and mix in the grated cheese. Season with salt and pepper and set aside.

Place a saucepan over a medium heat and add the milk, bay leaf and black peppercorns. Bring to the boil, add the fish and prawns, reduce the heat to low and poach for 4–5 minutes. Using a slotted spoon, transfer the fish to a plate and discard the bay leaf and peppercorns.

Place a clean saucepan over a low heat and melt the remaining butter, then whisk in the flour to make a thick paste or roux and cook for 3 minutes. Slowly whisk in the poaching milk and continue whisking until you reach a smooth consistency.

Next, whisk in the white wine and then simmer for 15 minutes, stirring occasionally. Stir in the mustard and chives, followed by the fish and prawns. Season with salt and pepper. Spoon the fish and sauce into the potato shells and top with the mashed potato and cheese mixture. Place them on a baking tray and bake for 20 minutes until piping hot and the cheesy mash is golden.

Serve with a sprinkling of chopped chives and a generous twist of freshly ground black pepper.

Fish Tacos with Pea Guacamole

SERVES 4

125g (4½oz) plain flour

¼ teaspoon cayenne pepper

1 medium free-range egg

250ml (9fl oz) light beer

250ml (9fl oz) sunflower oil

500g (1lb 2oz) skinless cod fillets, cut into 16 slices

8 small flour tortillas

125ml (4fl oz) soured cream

1 tablespoon sliced jalapeño chillies

75g (2½oz) white cabbage, shredded

30g (1oz) freshly chopped coriander

sea salt and freshly ground black pepper

FOR THE PEA GUACAMOLE

200g (7oz) fresh or frozen peas (thawed, if using frozen)

1 avocado, peeled and stoned

2 tablespoons freshly chopped mint

½ teaspoon chilli flakes

1 tablespoon crème fraîche

zest and juice of 1 lime, plus wedges to serve

Fish tacos are simple to make, in fact no more complicated than a hamburger. The cod in this dish is fried in strips and served in warm flour tortillas with creamy pea guacamole, cooling soured cream, refreshing lime and a nice kick of jalapeño chillies. In this recipe I use fish, but you can also fill the tacos with leftover roast chicken, pulled pork or strips of beef. When I am making these tacos for a Friday-night gathering, I serve the fried fish on a warmed platter, the warm tortillas on a hot plate, and the guacamole, jalapeño chillies, limes and soured cream in bowls to let everyone build their own.

Start by making the batter for the fish. Put the flour, cayenne pepper, a pinch of salt, the egg and beer in a large mixing bowl. Whisk together until you reach a smooth consistency and then set aside at room temperature.

Preheat the sunflower oil to 180°C (350°F) in a large pan. Dip the fish slices into the batter and allow the excess batter to drip off before adding to the oil. Fry the fish, flipping to ensure it is evenly browned, for about 4 minutes, then transfer to a kitchen-paper-lined plate and season with salt. Keep warm in a low oven while you prepare the rest of the dish.

Meanwhile, to make the pea guacamole, place all the ingredients in a food processor, season with salt and pepper and blend for a minute or until smooth. Transfer to a small serving dish.

Warm the tortillas in a dry frying pan. Serve the fried fish in the tortillas with the soured cream, jalapeños, cabbage, pea guacamole, fresh coriander and lime wedges.

Melt-in-the-Mouth Creamy Fennel & Fish Gratin

SERVES 4

25g (1oz) salted butter

2 fennel bulbs, halved and thinly sliced

4 skinless white fish fillets, such as hake or cod, weighing 800g (1lb 12oz) in total

200ml (7fl oz) double cream

½ teaspoon freshly grated nutmeg

1 tablespoon finely chopped fresh dill

100g (3½oz) Gruyère cheese, finely grated

sea salt and freshly ground black pepper

This dish couldn't be easier to make – it takes about 20 minutes to prepare and 20 minutes to cook. You can prepare this gratin the day before and then just pop it in the oven 20 minutes before you want to serve it. Fennel is the perfect partner for white fish as the aniseed taste lifts the flavour and the dill adds so much freshness. I love serving this dish with fluffy basmati rice and a green leaf salad.

Preheat the oven to 200°C/400°F/gas mark 6. Grease an 20cm (8in) square ovenproof dish with the butter.

Place the thinly sliced fennel in a layer on the bottom of the prepared dish, followed by the fish fillets and season with salt and pepper.

Whisk together the cream, nutmeg, dill and Gruyère cheese in a bowl and season to taste. Pour over the fish.

Bake for 20 minutes or until the top is golden and the fish is cooked.

Serve with a green salad, green beans or buttered spinach.

My Favourite Way to Roast Chicken

SERVES 4

100g (3½oz) salted butter, softened

2 garlic cloves, crushed

3 tablespoons finely chopped fresh herbs, such as flat-leaf parsley, thyme and rosemary

1 dessertspoon Dijon mustard

zest and juice of 1 lemon

1 whole chicken, weighing about 1.5kg (3lb 5oz)

4 sprigs of fresh rosemary

4 sprigs of fresh thyme

sea salt and freshly ground black pepper

This is the most watched IGTV recipe video that I have ever made. We all have our own favourite ways to roast chicken and are always so curious to see if there are any tips to make it that bit better. My top tip in this recipe is to spoon the flavoured butter up underneath the skin of the chicken breast – it transforms the flavour and moistness of the chicken. Serve with honey-roasted carrots and parsnips, mashed potato, gravy and mustard for a traditional chicken feast.

Preheat the oven to 200°C/400°F/gas mark 6.

Put the butter, garlic, chopped herbs and mustard in a bowl and mix together. Add the lemon zest and juice and season with salt and pepper. Mix together really well. Chop the used lemon into four pieces and set aside.

Place the chicken in a roasting tray and season the cavity. Place two of the lemon pieces in the cavity along with half the sprigs of rosemary and thyme – this will infuse the bird with flavour.

Arrange the bird so that the top of the legs and cavity are facing away from you, then carefully pull the skin up at the bottom of the chicken breasts and use a spoon or clean hands to get under the skin and gently separate the skin from the meat of the breast. Spoon two-thirds of the flavoured butter under the skin, smearing it around so that it covers as much of the chicken breasts as possible.

Smear the remaining flavoured butter over the outside of the chicken. Tuck the remaining sprigs of rosemary and thyme and the pieces of lemon around the chicken. Season with salt and pepper.

Roast for 1¼ hours or until the chicken is cooked through. The skin will be crispy and the meat will be flavoured with the delicious herbs, mustard, garlic and lemon.

Tent the chicken with foil and allow to rest for 30 minutes before carving.

Ricotta Meatballs with Polenta

SERVES 4

200g (7oz) minced beef

200g (7oz) minced pork

200g (7oz) ricotta cheese

2 onions, diced

4 garlic cloves, crushed

1 tablespoon finely chopped
fresh rosemary

80g (2¾oz) Parmesan
cheese, grated

40g (1½oz) fresh fine
breadcrumbs

1 medium free-range egg,
beaten

75g (2½oz) polenta

1–2 tablespoons olive oil

50g (1¾oz) salted butter,
plus 1 tablespoon (optional)

400g (14oz) cavolo nero,
roughly chopped

sea salt and freshly ground
black pepper

FOR THE ROSEMARY
TOMATO SAUCE

1 tablespoon olive oil

1 onion, thinly sliced

2 garlic cloves, crushed

1 teaspoon finely chopped
fresh rosemary

400g (14oz) can cherry
tomatoes

1 tablespoon tomato purée

This is the traditional way that they make meatballs in Sicily.
I mix together minced pork and ricotta with the ground beef
– the pork brings flavour and juiciness and the ricotta brings
a lovely lightness. I serve them with polenta as they do during
the colder months in Italy, but you could use spaghetti. This
is a great freezer recipe, so make double and you can store it
away. It's nice to serve a green vegetable alongside to lighten the
dish; I use cavolo nero but you could choose purple sprouting
broccoli, shredded cabbage or a green salad.

Place the beef, pork, ricotta, onions, garlic, rosemary, Parmesan, breadcrumbs
and beaten egg in a bowl and season with salt and pepper. Mix well. Using
your hands, shape into 30 meatballs, and transfer to a plate. Cover with
clingfilm and place in the fridge for 1 hour to set so that they don't crumble
during cooking. You can also leave the meatballs in the fridge for up to
3 days or freeze them for up to a month until you are ready to cook them.

While the meatballs are chilling, make the rosemary tomato sauce. Place a
saucepan over a low heat and add the oil, then stir in the onion, garlic and
rosemary and simmer for 2 minutes. Add the tomatoes and tomato purée,
season with salt and pepper and cook for 15 minutes, stirring occasionally.

Next, get the polenta cooking. Pour 600ml (20fl oz) water into a saucepan
over a medium heat and season with salt and pepper. Once the water has
come to the boil, whisk in the polenta. Reduce the heat, cover and cook
for about 25 minutes, stirring every 5 minutes. Once it has cooked, stir in
a tablespoon of olive oil or butter.

Now back to the meatballs. Place a frying pan over a medium heat and pour
in 1 tablespoon of olive oil, add the meatballs and brown on all sides. Then
spoon the meatballs into the tomato rosemary sauce and cook for 15 minutes.

Place the cavolo nero in a pan over a medium heat with the butter and
season with salt and pepper. Cook for 5 minutes, turning the leaves with
tongs so they cook evenly.

Divide the polenta between four warmed bowls, followed by the meatballs,
an extra spoonful of the rosemary tomato sauce and the cavolo nero. Serve.

Steak with Creamy Mushroom Linguine

SERVES 4

2 sirloin steaks, weighing 300g (10½oz) each

400g (14oz) linguine

1 tablespoon olive oil

FOR THE CREAMY MUSHROOM SAUCE

1 tablespoon olive oil

1 onion, diced

2 garlic cloves, crushed

200g (7oz) chestnut mushrooms, sliced

1 tablespoon freshly chopped rosemary, plus extra to garnish

juice of ½ lemon

200ml (7fl oz) double cream

sea salt and freshly ground black pepper

This charred juicy steak wrapped with silky pasta and creamy, nutty mushrooms with flavours of garlic and rosemary is one of my favourite dishes to serve when I have people for supper and also when it's just the two of us. You can make the creamy mushroom sauce ahead, swap out the rosemary for tarragon or thyme and use spaghetti or pappardelle too. I like to serve a refreshing green leaf salad afterwards to cleanse the palate after the cream.

Remove the steaks from the fridge 30 minutes before cooking to allow them to come up to room temperature.

To make the creamy mushroom sauce, place a frying pan over a medium heat and add the oil. Then stir in the onion and garlic and cook for 2 minutes. Add the mushrooms, season with salt and pepper and continue to cook for 10 minutes, tossing every minute or so. Add the fresh rosemary and lemon juice and cook for a further minute. Pour in the cream, stir, reduce the heat to low and cook for 5 minutes. Keep warm over a low heat.

Meanwhile, put a large saucepan of salted boiling water over a high heat, stir in the pasta and cook for 10 minutes or until al dente. Drain, reserving a couple of tablespoons of the cooking water.

To cook the steaks, heat a griddle or frying pan over a high heat until smoking hot. Lightly brush the steaks with the olive oil and season with salt and pepper. Place the prepared steaks in the hot pan and cook to the following times: BLUE: 1 minute each side; RARE: 1½ minutes each side; MEDIUM RARE: 2 minutes each side; MEDIUM: 2¼ minutes each side; MEDIUM-WELL DONE: 2½–3 minutes each side.

Leave the steaks to rest for about 2 minutes before serving to allow the juices that have been drawn to the surface to relax back into the meat.

Return the cooked pasta back to the large saucepan over a low heat with the reserved pasta cooking water and the creamy mushroom sauce. Toss together and serve in warmed dishes. Thinly slice the steaks and serve on top of the creamy mushroom linguine, scattered with some chopped rosemary and a twist of black pepper.

Chicken, Mushroom & Kale Pie

SERVES 4

30g (1oz) salted butter

4 skinless chicken breasts, diced

1 leek, finely sliced

280g (10oz) button mushrooms, quartered

200g (7oz) kale, sliced

1 tablespoon plain flour, plus extra for dusting

250ml (9fl oz) whole milk

100ml (3½fl oz) single cream

500g (1lb 2oz) ready-made puff pastry (use butter puff or brush ordinary puff with a little melted butter)

1 medium free-range egg, beaten

fresh thyme leaves

sea salt and freshly ground black pepper

On a chilly evening this is absolute heaven! You can make the filling a day ahead and then just assemble the pie with the pastry a couple of hours before you wish to serve it. The creamy filling with the nutty flavours from the mushrooms and freshness from the leeks and kale is delicious. You can add your own signature to the filling by mixing in a tablespoon of finely chopped tarragon, thyme, marjoram or rosemary. I like to serve steamed broccoli, asparagus, green beans or a green leaf salad alongside the pie.

Preheat the oven to 200°C/400°F/gas mark 6.

Set a large saucepan over a medium heat and melt the butter. Add the chicken, season with salt and pepper and cook for 5 minutes. Stir in the leek and cook for a further minute. Add the mushrooms and kale and cook for 3 minutes. Sprinkle over the flour, stir and cook for a minute, then pour in the milk and cream and cook for 10 minutes, stirring, until the sauce has thickened. Remove from the heat and set aside.

Roll out the pastry on a lightly floured work surface and cut it into four pieces big enough to cover four small pie dishes. Spoon the chicken mixture into the four individual pie dishes and brush the rims with beaten egg. Lift the pastry onto the pies, trimming off any excess. Press down and crimp the edges with a fork. Cut a couple of slits in the pastry lids to let the steam escape and brush all over with the remaining beaten egg and sprinkle the thyme leaves on top. Bake for 15–20 minutes or until the pastry is crisp and golden brown. Alternatively you can make this in one large baking dish and bake for 30 minutes

Serve with any of the suggestions above.

Classic Italian Pork & Beef Ragù

SERVES 6

2 tablespoons olive oil

1 onion, finely diced

1 carrot, peeled and finely diced

½ celery stick, finely diced

4 garlic cloves, crushed

500g (1lb 2oz) minced pork

500g (1lb 2oz) minced beef

400ml (14fl oz) red wine

600g (1lb 5oz) canned cherry tomatoes

2 tablespoons tomato purée

2 teaspoons dried oregano

1 teaspoon freshly grated nutmeg

hot beef stock (optional)

800g (1lb 12oz) pappardelle

100g (3½oz) Parmesan cheese, grated

sea salt and freshly ground black pepper

Everyone loves ragù, or bolognese as we call it – it's a real crowd-pleaser. This is a great make-ahead recipe, so try to cook it at your leisure the day or morning before as it always tastes better when it's been cooked a few hours before serving. I make it with half pork and half beef – the minced beef alone makes for a coarse chunky sauce, but adding the pork makes it sweeter and fuller in flavour. I always double up the recipe as it freezes so well. Delicious served with pappardelle as here, it is also perfect with linguine or spaghetti, and of course lots of freshly grated Parmesan cheese on top.

Place an ovenproof casserole dish over a medium heat and add the oil. Stir in the onion, carrot, celery and garlic and cook for 5 minutes or until softened. Add the pork and beef and season with salt and pepper. Cook, stirring occasionally, until the meat has turned a light brown colour.

Pour in the red wine and leave to simmer for about 5 minutes. Stir in the tomatoes, tomato purée, dried oregano and nutmeg, season with salt and pepper and mix well. Reduce the heat to low and simmer for 1 hour, stirring occasionally. The longer you let it simmer the more tender and flavoursome the ragù becomes. Add a little hot beef stock if it becomes too thick.

Put a large saucepan of salted water over a high heat and bring to the boil. Tip in the pasta and stir for 2 minutes. Cook according to the packet instructions until al dente and then drain, reserving 2 tablespoons of the cooking water.

Return the pasta to the saucepan (off the heat) and stir in the reserved cooking water followed by the ragù. Serve topped with the grated Parmesan.

Marsala & Star Anise Poached Pears

I created this recipe after the first harvest of honey from our beehives, when the pears were ripe and ready to be picked from the orchard, and it's become an autumn favourite. At other times of year, I swap out the pears for whatever fruits are in season, such as peaches or plums. Marsala wine is a must for your pantry as it's so good for poaching fruit, adding a delicious rich sweetness, and the star anise brings a deep flavour of aniseed to the dish.

SERVES 4

250ml (9fl oz) dry Marsala wine

100g (3½oz) light soft brown sugar

2 tablespoons runny local honey

1 tablespoon freshly squeezed lemon juice

3 star anise

1 cinnamon stick, broken in half

4 pears, peeled with the stem still attached

200g (7oz) mascarpone cheese, to serve

Start by making the spiced marsala syrup. Place the Marsala wine, sugar, honey, lemon juice, star anise and cinnamon in a saucepan. Bring to the boil, then reduce the heat to low and place the pears in the pan so that they stand upright. Cover the pan and cook for 15 minutes, basting the pears with the liquid a couple of times during cooking, until the pears can easily be pierced with a fork.

Scoop the pears onto serving dishes, pour the syrup on top and serve each portion with a dollop of mascarpone.

Cardamom Panna Cotta with Rhubarb

There are several fantastic things about panna cotta. Firstly, you can make them a day ahead, and secondly you can add your own signature by including different flavours and fruit depending on the season. In the spring and early summer, we have an abundance of rhubarb growing in the garden, then I switch to fresh berries in the middle of the summer, and figs and pears in the autumn. Cardamom is such a wonderful ingredient – it brings citrus, mint, and spice to the panna cotta. You can also swap it with a couple of teaspoons of rosewater or orange blossom water.

SERVES 4

FOR THE PANNA COTTA

250ml (9fl oz) double cream

½ teaspoon cardamom pods, crushed

25g (1oz) caster sugar

2 gelatine leaves

250ml (9fl oz) whole milk

FOR THE POACHED RHUBARB

2 sticks of rhubarb, cut into 2.5cm (1in) pieces

80g (2¾oz) caster sugar

To make the panna cotta, pour the cream into a saucepan, add the cardamom pods and sugar and bring to the boil, then simmer until reduced by a third.

Soak the gelatine in the milk for about 15 minutes or until soft. Remove the gelatine, heat the milk until boiling, then return the gelatine to the milk and stir until dissolved. Pour the milk and gelatine mixture into the cooked cream, stir and then strain through a sieve (to catch the cardamom pods). Pour the liquid into four serving glasses. Leave to cool completely, then cover with clingfilm and place in the fridge for at least 1 hour to set.

Meanwhile, make the poached rhubarb. Place the chopped rhubarb, sugar and 50ml (2fl oz) water into a saucepan over a medium heat. Cook for 5 minutes, then reduce the heat to low and continue to cook for a further 10 minutes until tender but still holding its shape. Set aside and leave to cool.

Remove the panna cotta from the fridge about 30 minutes before serving so that they warm up a little. Spoon some poached rhubarb on top of each panna cotta and serve.

Classic Tiramisu

I think tiramisu has to be my all-time favourite dessert, and this is my top way to make it. I am not going to give any alternatives because, for me, adding fruit or other flavours just takes away from this perfect pudding – creamy with thin layers of velvet chocolate and notes of coffee throughout. You can make these individual desserts a day ahead.

SERVES 4

3 medium free-range egg yolks

80g (2¾oz) caster sugar

450g (1lb) mascarpone cheese

200ml (7fl oz) strong brewed coffee or espresso, cold

14 boudoir biscuits (ladyfingers)

150g (5½oz) cocoa powder, plus extra to serve

Using an electric whisk, beat the egg yolks and caster sugar together in a large bowl until pale and thick. Add the mascarpone and whisk slowly until the mixture is pale and smooth. Stir in 50ml (2fl oz) of the coffee until completely combined.

Dip half the boudoir biscuits into the remaining coffee. Place equal amounts into the bottom of four glass coffee cups or small serving bowls. Alternatively, put the ingredients in a single glass bowl to make one large tiramisu. Spoon over half the coffee-mascarpone mixture and sprinkle with half the cocoa powder. Repeat with the remaining coffee-dipped biscuits, coffee-mascarpone and cocoa powder. Cover with clingfilm and chill in the fridge for 2 hours, then dust with a little extra cocoa powder before serving.

Quick Rosewater Chocolate Mousses

This is my go-to dessert when I have very little time to make anything, but I still want to give everyone a treat. You can swap out the rosewater for vanilla or coffee extract, or cardamom. These take just 15 minutes to prepare and 15 minutes to chill, and you can make them a day ahead.

SERVES 4

100g (3½oz) dark chocolate (at least 70 per cent cocoa solids), broken into pieces

75g (2½oz) caster sugar

1 tablespoon rosewater

2 medium free-range eggs

250g (9oz) mascarpone cheese

Place the dark chocolate in a heatproof bowl set over a saucepan of simmering water and allow it to melt, then remove from the heat. Stir in the caster sugar and rosewater and crack in the eggs. Using a hand-held electric beater, whisk for 5 minutes. Finally, whisk in the mascarpone for a few seconds, until smooth.

Divide between four 250ml (9fl oz) serving glasses and chill in the fridge for 15 minutes before serving.

Lemon Cheesecake

This was the most searched-for recipe on my website last summer! I made it on my IGTV and I couldn't believe the number of people who made it and tagged me. We all love a good cheesecake and I think this one is such a winner because the lemon cream topping is so light, citrusy and fluffy, with a perfect buttery biscuit base. This can be made a couple of days in advance and you can use this exact recipe to make a lime version by just swapping out the lemons for limes.

SERVES 8

250g (9oz) digestive biscuits

80g (2¾oz) whole hazelnuts (or almonds, walnuts or chocolate nibs)

100g (3½oz) butter, melted

300ml (10fl oz) double cream

150g (5½oz) caster sugar

340g (11¾oz) cream cheese

zest of 3 lemons, juice of 2, plus extra zest to serve (optional)

edible flowers, to decorate (optional)

Line the base of a 18cm (7in) springform cake tin with greaseproof paper.

Blitz the digestive biscuits and hazelnuts in a blender until you get a breadcrumb-like consistency. Pour in the melted butter and blend for 30 seconds. Spoon the mixture into the prepared tin and use the back of the spoon to smooth it flat. Put the tin into the fridge to chill while you make the topping.

Whip the cream using a whisk or mixer, then once the cream is whipped, add the sugar, cream cheese and lemon zest and juice and whisk together until light and fluffy.

Remove the springform cake tin from the fridge and spoon in the lemon mixture. Use the back of a spoon to smooth out the top. Return the cheesecake to the fridge for at least 2 hours to set fully. Remove from the fridge 30 minutes before serving.

I like to finish off the cheesecake by decorating it with some edible flowers and an extra sprinkling of lemon zest.

Peach Tarte Tatin
with Orange Blossom Cream

This is so gorgeous, caramelized ripe peaches on a crisp thin pastry base served with a decadent orange blossom cream! If you don't have orange blossom water just use the zest of an orange instead. You can make this a couple of hours before serving, and leave it to rest at room temperature (not in the fridge). It's also delicious made with apples, pineapple or pears.

SERVES 6

150g (5½oz) caster sugar

70g (2½oz) unsalted butter

½ vanilla pod, cut in half lengthways

6 peaches, halved and stoned

325g (11½oz) ready-made puff pastry

FOR THE ORANGE BLOSSOM CREAM

250g (9oz) crème fraîche

2 tablespoons orange blossom water

1 tablespoon orange zest

Preheat the oven to 180°C/350°F/gas mark 4.

Place a cast-iron pan or an ovenproof frying pan over a low heat and add the caster sugar and 100ml (3½fl oz) water. Stir until the sugar has dissolved. Once the sugar has dissolved, increase the heat to high and simmer for 12–14 minutes or until the syrup is a light golden-brown colour. Stir in the butter and scrape in the seeds from the vanilla pod, then cook for a further 2–3 minutes or until you reach a caramel consistency.

Arrange the halved peaches, cut-side up, over the caramel.

Roll out the puff pastry so that it covers the peaches in the pan. Place the pastry on top of the peaches and fold the edges down the sides so that you're tucking in the peaches. Make three small slits in the centre of the pastry with a sharp knife and bake for 45 minutes until the peaches are caramelized and the pastry is golden.

Meanwhile, to make the orange blossom cream, whisk the crème fraîche with the orange blossom water and orange zest and set aside.

When the tarte tatin is cooked, carefully invert the tarte out onto a serving dish. Slice and serve with a dollop of the orange blossom cream.

Vegan Chocolate Tart with Hazelnut Crust

This moreish vegan chocolate tart is so decadent and rich. The crumbly crust is a blend of nuts, oats, coconut oil and maple syrup, and the filling is so silky that the textures work really well together. You can make this a couple of days ahead, and serve small slices as it is quite rich.

SERVES 6

vegetable oil, for greasing

100g (3½oz) hazelnut flour or ground hazelnuts

300g (10½oz) rolled oats

5 tablespoons coconut oil, melted

4 tablespoons maple syrup

100g (3½oz) whole hazelnuts, roughly chopped

FOR THE FILLING

400g (14oz) can coconut milk

150g (5½oz) vegan dark chocolate (at least 70 per cent cocoa solids), broken into pieces

80ml (2¾fl oz) maple syrup

70g (2½oz) hazelnut butter

1 teaspoon vanilla extract

pinch of sea salt

Preheat the oven to 180°C/350°F/gas mark 4. Lightly brush a 23cm (9in) loose-bottomed tart tin with vegetable oil and set aside.

Place the hazelnut flour or ground hazelnuts, oats, coconut oil and maple syrup in a food processor and mix until well combined. The mixture should be sticky when you press it between your fingers. Transfer the dough to the prepared tart tin. Using your fingers, press the dough down evenly to cover the base of the tin. Bake for 15–17 minutes until golden brown, then remove from the oven and leave to cool completely.

Add all the filling ingredients to a saucepan over a medium heat and mix until the chocolate begins to melt. (Make sure to mix often so the chocolate doesn't burn!) Mix until combined, then pour the mixture evenly into the baked tart case. Transfer the tart to the fridge for 2–3 hours until the filling is set.

Remove the tart from the tin and top with the chopped hazelnuts and serve. Store any leftovers in an airtight container in the fridge for up to a week.

Carrot Cake with Orange Blossom Icing

MAKES 1 x 23cm (9in) LOAF
CAKE/SERVES 10

3 medium free-range eggs

140ml (4½fl oz) vegetable
oil, plus extra for greasing

225g (8oz) soft light brown
sugar

1 teaspoon ground cinnamon

1 teaspoon freshly grated
nutmeg

350g (12oz) grated carrots
(grated weight)

100g (3½oz) golden raisins

100g (3½oz) walnuts,
chopped

200g (7oz) self-raising flour

½ teaspoon bicarbonate
of soda

FOR THE ORANGE
BLOSSOM ICING

300g (10½oz) cream
cheese, chilled

70g (2½oz) unsalted butter,
at room temperature

300g (10½oz) icing sugar,
sifted

2 teaspoons orange blossom
water

zest of 1 orange, plus extra
to decorate (optional)

This was my most requested cake when I had restaurants in Dublin a few years ago. It's incredibly simple to make – the cake itself is deliciously moist with wonderful hints of cinnamon and nutmeg, and it is topped with a dreamy orange blossom icing – utter heaven! If you are finding it hard to get your hands on orange blossom water, then use the zest of an orange instead. The cake will keep for one week in an airtight container and it also freezes really well without the icing.

Preheat the oven to 180°C/350°F/gas mark 4 and oil and line a 13 x 23cm (5 x 9in) loaf tin with greaseproof paper.

Beat the eggs in a large bowl, then add the oil, brown sugar, cinnamon, nutmeg, grated carrots, raisins and chopped walnuts and stir to combine.

Sift in the remaining dry ingredients and bring the mixture together using a wooden or large metal spoon until well combined. Transfer the mixture into the prepared loaf tin and smooth the surface. Bake for 1¼ hours or until a skewer inserted into the middle comes out clean.

Leave the cake to cool in the tin for about 5 minutes before turning out onto a wire rack and leaving to cool completely.

To make the icing, beat the cream cheese and butter together in a bowl until well combined. Add the icing sugar, orange blossom water and orange zest and mix until the icing is smooth and thick. Using a palette knife, spread the icing evenly over the top of the cooled cake, dipping the knife into a bowl of hot water if the icing is hard to spread.

Decorate with a sprinkling of orange zest, if you wish.

Strawberry & Elderflower Sorbet

SERVES 6

600g (1lb 5oz) strawberries, hulled and halved, plus extra, chopped, to serve

250ml (9fl oz) elderflower cordial

zest and juice of 1 lemon

When strawberries are ripe and juicy, this is the most refreshing dessert to serve on a warm evening. At the beginning of the summer when the elderflowers are in season, I always take a weekend out to forage for them and make big batches of elderflower cordial. You can watch me forage and make the cordial on my IGTV.

Place the strawberries, elderflower cordial, 150ml (5fl oz) water and the lemon zest and juice in a food processor and blend for 3 minutes until smooth.

Pour the mixture through a sieve into a freezerproof container, pushing all the delicious juice through the sieve using the back of a spoon. Chill for 1 hour in the fridge.

Pour the chilled mixture into an ice-cream maker and churn for 20 minutes or follow your manufacturer's instructions. Scoop it back into the freezerproof container and transfer to the freezer for 2 hours until firm.

Remove from the freezer 10 minutes before serving, as this makes it easier to scoop. Serve in scoops with chopped fresh strawberries.

Index

A

aioli, fresh dill 54
almonds: aromatic lamb & sweet
  potato casserole 68
  cauliflower & almond rice 79
  chicken tagine 61
  honey-roasted carrots with torn
  burrata & salsa rustica 82
apples: harvest salad with kale, apple,
  beetroot & grilled halloumi 76
aromatic lamb & sweet potato casse
  role 68
aubergines: Sicilian aubergine stew
  with cauliflower & almond rice 79
avocados: green gazpacho 17
  pea guacamole 144
  prawn cocktail 23

B

basil: basil pesto 10
  Margherita risotto 118
  mint & basil yogurt dip 90
beans: Bella bean casserole 51
  Mexican bean salad 106
  three-bean chilli 136–7
Béarnaise sauce 40
beef: Italian pork & beef ragù 154
  ricotta meatballs with polenta
  149
  steak frites & 10-minute Béarnaise 40
  steak with creamy mushroom linguine
  150
beetroot: harvest salad with kale,
  apple, beetroot & grilled halloumi 76
Bella bean casserole 51
black beans: Mexican bean salad 106
black-eyed beans: three-bean chilli
  136–7
boudoir biscuits (ladyfingers): tiramisu
  162
bread: creamed mushrooms on toast 111
  French onion soup with Gruyère
  toasts 47
  garlic & chilli prawn toasts 27
broths see soups
bulgur tabbouleh with grilled
  vegetables 110
buona amatriciana 41
burrata: honey-roasted carrots with
  torn burrata & salsa rustica 82
butter: lemon & caper butter 24
  sage butter 78
butter chicken curry 133
butternut squash: chickpea, spinach &
  butternut squash stew 119

C

Caesar salad, kale 85
cake: carrot cake with orange blossom
  icing 170
cannellini beans: Bella bean casserole 51
  garlic lamb cutlets with crushed
  rosemary cannellini beans 130
  Mexican bean salad 106
capers: lemon & caper butter 24
  sea bass ceviche with lime, chilli &
  capers 21
  tuna, lemon & caper pasta 126
carbonara, roast butternut squash 112
cardamom panna cotta with rhubarb 161
carrots: carrot cake with orange
  blossom icing 170
  honey-roasted carrots with torn
  burrata & salsa rustica 82
  sunshine salad 107
  sunshine soup 99
casseroles: aromatic lamb & sweet
  potato casserole 68
  Bella bean casserole 51
  see also stews; tagines
cauliflower: cauliflower & almond
  rice 79
  cauliflower cheese baked potato 75
  coconut, cauliflower & chickpea
  curry 72
  kimchi cauliflower fried rice 95
cavolo nero: kale Caesar salad 85
  ricotta meatballs with polenta
  149
ceviche, sea bass 21
cheese: buona amatriciana 41
  cauliflower cheese baked potato 75
  cheese soufflé tart with walnut-
  crusted pastry 140
  chickpea Greek salad with herby
  lemon dressing 48
  crispy galette with butternut squash,
  feta & olives 19
  foolproof three cheese soufflé 50
  French onion soup with Gruyère
  toasts 47
  gooey Gruyère omelette 14
  harvest salad with kale, apple,
  beetroot & grilled halloumi 76
  herby cheese-crusted chicken kiev 63
  honey-roasted carrots with torn
  burrata & salsa rustica 82
  Italian pork & beef ragù 154
  kale Caesar salad 85
  Margherita risotto 118
  melt-in-the-mouth creamy fennel &
  fish gratin 146

  crispy galette with butternut squash,
  feta & olives 19
  roast butternut squash carbonara 112
  Thai curry noodles 92

pasta amore 116
  roast pumpkin, mozzarella & chilli 86
  spinach, leek & feta filo tart 123
  see also mascarpone cheese; ricotta
cheesecake, lemon 165
chicken: butter chicken curry 133
  chicken Florentine 35
  chicken, mushroom & kale pie 153
  chicken noodle soup 37
  chicken tagine 61
  herby cheese-crusted chicken kiev 63
  mustard, honey & tarragon chicken
  traybake with shallots & parsnips 62
  my favourite way to roast chicken 147
  Spanish chicken & rice 64
  spiced chicken & chickpea curry 58
chickpeas: Bella bean casserole 51
  chickpea Greek salad with herby
  lemon dressing 48
  chickpea, spinach & butternut
  squash stew 119
  coconut & spinach dal 121
  coconut, cauliflower & chickpea
  curry 72
  four ways with baked sweet
  potatoes & hummus 109
  spiced chicken & chickpea curry 58
chillies: garlic & chilli prawn toasts 27
  noodle soup with chilli, ginger &
  green vegetables 122
  prawn, chilli & lemon linguine 127
  roast pumpkin, mozzarella & chilli 86
  sea bass ceviche with lime, chilli &
  capers 21
  three-bean chilli 136–7
chips: steak frites 40
chocolate: quick rosewater chocolate
  mousses 164
  tiramisu 162
  vegan chocolate tart with hazelnut
  crust 168
chorizo: creamy chorizo & garlic
  mussels 55
  Spanish chicken & rice 64
clams: clam linguine 34
  Montauk seafood pot 56
coconut milk: coconut & spinach dal 121
  coconut, cauliflower & chickpea
  curry 72
  Indian coconut & tomato fish curry
  129
  prawn laksa with rice noodles 124
  Thai curry noodles 92
  vegan chocolate tart with hazelnut
  crust 168
coffee: tiramisu 162
corn on the cob: Montauk seafood
  pot 56
courgettes: courgette fritters with
  mint & basil yogurt dip 90
  sunshine salad 107

crab: crab cakes with fresh dill aioli 54
ginger & preserved lemon crab
spaghetti 32
cream: baked eggs with ham, cream,
nutmeg & thyme 38
cardamom panna cotta with rhubarb
161
creamed mushrooms on toast 111
lemon cheesecake 165
melt-in-the-mouth creamy fennel &
fish gratin 146
spinach, leek & feta filo tart 123
steak with creamy mushroom
linguine 150
cream cheese: lemon cheesecake 165
orange blossom icing 170
crème fraîche: orange blossom cream
167
cucumber: bulgur tabbouleh with
grilled vegetables 110
chickpea Greek salad with herby
lemon dressing 48
green gazpacho 17
curry: butter chicken curry 133
coconut & spinach dal 121
coconut, cauliflower & chickpea
curry 72
Indian coconut & tomato fish curry
129
prawn laksa with rice noodles 124
spiced chicken & chickpea curry 58
Thai curry noodles 92

D
dal, coconut & spinach 121
digestive biscuits: lemon cheesecake
165
dill: fresh dill aioli 54
hash browns with dill fried eggs &
harissa 105
dips: harissa dip 81
mint & basil yogurt dip 90
dressings: herby lemon dressing 48
lime dressing 106
my everyday salad dressing 11

E
eggs: baked eggs with ham, cream,
nutmeg & thyme 38
classic tiramisu 162
egg-fried rice with green vegetables
20
fresh dill aioli 54
gooey Gruyère omelette 14
hash browns with dill fried eggs &
harissa 105
huevos rancheros 89
salmon niçoise 28
elderflower cordial: strawberry &
elderflower sorbet 171

F
falafels, sweet potato 81
fennel: melt-in-the-mouth creamy
fennel & fish gratin 146
15-minute pan-fried plaice with lemon
& caper butter 24
filo pastry: crispy galette with
butternut squash, feta & olives 19
spinach, leek & feta filo tart 123
fish: 15-minute pan-fried plaice with
lemon & caper butter 24
fish pie baked potatoes 143
fish tacos with salsa & pea guacamole
144
Indian coconut & tomato fish curry
129
melt-in-the-mouth creamy fennel &
fish gratin 146
potato cakes with smoked salmon 26
salmon niçoise 28
sea bass ceviche with lime, chilli &
capers 21
sea bass & spring onion in a wild
garlic broth 141
Spanish fish stew 52
tuna, lemon & caper pasta 126
foolproof three cheese soufflé 50
French beans: Indian coconut &
tomato fish curry 129
noodle soup with chilli, ginger &
green vegetables 122
salmon niçoise 28
French onion soup with Gruyère
toasts 47
fritters, courgette 90

G
galette: crispy galette with butternut
squash, feta & olives 19
garlic: creamy chorizo & garlic
mussels 55
garlic & chilli prawn toasts 27
garlic lamb cutlets with crushed
rosemary cannellini beans 130
herby cheese-crusted chicken kiev 63
slow-cooked squid with olives,
tomatoes & garlic 31
gazpacho, green 17
ginger: ginger & preserved lemon crab
spaghetti 32
noodle soup with chilli, ginger &
green vegetables 122
vegetable wonton & ginger broth 96
gnocchi, sweet potato 78
gooey Gruyère omelette 14
gratin, melt-in-the-mouth creamy
fennel & fish 146
Greek salad, chickpea 48
green gazpacho 17
gremolata, creamy polenta with green
vegetables & 100

guacamole, pea 144

H
halloumi, harvest salad with kale,
apple, beetroot & grilled 76
ham: baked eggs with ham, cream,
nutmeg & thyme 38
pineapple glazed ham 66
harissa: harissa dip 81
hash browns with dill fried eggs &
harissa 105
harvest salad with kale, apple,
beetroot & grilled halloumi 76
hash browns with dill fried eggs &
harissa 105
hazelnut flour: vegan chocolate tart
with hazelnut crust 168
hazelnuts: flat-leaf parsley pesto 99
lemon cheesecake 165
herbs: herby cheese-crusted chicken
kiev 63
herby lemon dressing 48
hollandaise sauce 11
huevos rancheros 89
hummus, four ways with baked sweet
potatoes & 109

I
icing, orange blossom 170
Indian coconut & tomato fish curry 129
Italian pork & beef ragù 154

K
kale: chicken, mushroom & kale pie 153
harvest salad with kale, apple,
beetroot & grilled halloumi 76
kale Caesar salad 85
kidney beans: Mexican bean salad 106
three-bean chilli with all the
trimmings 136–7
kiev, herby cheese-crusted chicken 63
kimchi cauliflower fried rice 95

L
laksa, prawn 124
lamb: aromatic lamb & sweet potato
casserole 68
garlic lamb cutlets with crushed
rosemary cannellini beans 130
lamb chops with crushed peas, mint
jus & pan-fried potatoes 42
leeks: mushroom, leek & thyme
risotto 91
spinach, leek & feta filo tart 123
spring green pearl barley risotto 115
lemons: ginger & preserved lemon
crab spaghetti 32
herby lemon dressing 48
lemon & caper butter 24
lemon cheesecake 165
prawn, chilli & lemon linguine 127

tuna, lemon & caper pasta 126
lentils: coconut & spinach dal 121
lettuce: kale Caesar salad 85
  prawn cocktail 23
limes: lime dressing 106
  sea bass ceviche with lime, chilli &
    capers 21
linguine: clam linguine 34
  prawn, chilli & lemon linguine 127
  steak with creamy mushroom
    linguine 150

M
Margherita risotto 118
Marsala & star anise poached pears 158
mascarpone: Marsala & star anise
  poached pears 158
  quick rosewater chocolate mousses
    164
  tiramisu 162
meatballs, ricotta 149
melt-in-the-mouth creamy fennel &
  fish gratin 146
Mexican bean salad 106
mint: lamb chops with crushed peas,
  mint jus & pan-fried potatoes 42
  mint & basil yogurt dip 90
Montauk seafood pot 56
mousses, quick rosewater
  chocolate 164
mushrooms: chicken Florentine 35
  chicken, mushroom & kale pie 153
  creamed mushrooms on toast 111
  creamy polenta with green
    vegetables & gremolata 100
  mushroom, leek & thyme risotto 91
  steak with creamy mushroom
    linguine 150
mussels: creamy chorizo & garlic
  mussels 55
  Montauk seafood pot 56
my everyday salad dressing 11
my favourite way to roast chicken 147

N
niçoise salad, salmon 28
noodles: chicken noodle soup 37
  noodle soup with chilli, ginger &
    green vegetables 122
  prawn laksa 124
  Thai curry noodles 92

O
olives: chickpea Greek salad with
  herby lemon dressing 48
  crispy galette with butternut squash,
    feta & olives 19
  Sicilian aubergine stew with
    cauliflower & almond rice 79
  slow-cooked squid with olives,
    tomatoes & garlic 31

Spanish chicken & rice 64
omelette, gooey Gruyère 14
onions: French onion soup with
  Gruyère toasts 47
orange blossom water: orange
  blossom cream 167
  orange blossom icing 170

P
pak choi: chicken noodle soup 37
pancetta: buona amatriciana 41
  roast butternut squash carbonara 112
panna cotta, cardamom 161
parsley: flat-leaf parsley pesto 99
  gremolata 100
parsnips, mustard, honey & tarragon
  chicken traybake with shallots & 62
pasta: buona amatriciana 41
  clam linguine 34
  ginger & preserved lemon crab
    spaghetti 32
  Italian pork & beef ragù 154
  pasta amore 116
  prawn, chilli & lemon linguine 127
  roast butternut squash carbonara 112
  steak with creamy mushroom
    linguine 150
  tuna, lemon & caper pasta 126
pastry, walnut-crusted 140
peach tarte tatin 167
pearl barley risotto, spring green 115
pears, Marsala & star anise poached
  158
peas: creamy polenta with green
  vegetables & gremolata 100
  Indian coconut & tomato fish curry
    129
  pea guacamole 144
  lamb chops with crushed peas, mint
    jus & pan-fried potatoes 42
  spring green pearl barley risotto 115
peppercorns: pepper sauce 11
peppers: green gazpacho 17
  huevos rancheros 89
  Mexican bean salad 106
  Spanish chicken & rice 64
pesto: basil pesto 10
  flat-leaf parsley pesto 99
pie, chicken, mushroom & kale 153
pine nuts: basil pesto 10
pineapple glazed ham 66
pizza, ricotta, honey & thyme 139
plaice: 15-minute pan-fried plaice with
  lemon & caper butter 24
polenta: creamy polenta with green
  vegetables & gremolata 100
  ricotta meatballs with polenta
    149
pork: classic Italian pork & beef ragù 154
  crispy mustard breaded pork chops
    with sweet potato wedges 69

ricotta meatballs with polenta
  149
potatoes: cauliflower cheese baked
  potato 75
  fish pie baked potatoes 143
  hash browns with dill fried eggs &
    harissa 105
  lamb chops with crushed peas, mint
    jus & pan-fried potatoes 42
  Montauk seafood pot 56
  potato cakes with smoked salmon 26
  salmon niçoise 28
  steak frites 40
prawns: fish pie baked potatoes 143
  garlic & chilli prawn toasts 27
  Montauk seafood pot 56
  prawn, chilli & lemon linguine 127
  prawn cocktail 23
  prawn laksa with rice noodles 124
puff pastry: chicken, mushroom &
  kale pie 153
  peach tarte tatin with orange
    blossom cream 167
pumpkin: roast pumpkin, mozzarella
  & chilli 86
pumpkin seeds: kale Caesar salad 85
purple sprouting broccoli: creamy
  polenta with green vegetables &
    gremolata 100
  noodle soup with chilli, ginger &
    green vegetables 122

R
ragù, Italian pork & beef 154
raisins: aromatic lamb & sweet potato
  casserole 68
  carrot cake with orange blossom
    icing 170
rhubarb, cardamom panna cotta with
  161
rice: cauliflower & almond rice 79
  egg-fried rice with green vegetables
    20
  harvest salad with kale, apple,
beetroot & grilled halloumi 76
  kimchi cauliflower fried rice 95
  Margherita risotto 118
  mushroom, leek & thyme risotto 91
  Spanish chicken & rice 64
ricotta: ricotta, honey & thyme pizza
  139
  ricotta meatballs with polenta 149
risotto: Margherita risotto 118
  mushroom, leek & thyme risotto 91
  spring green pearl barley risotto 115
rosemary: garlic lamb cutlets with
  crushed rosemary cannellini beans
    130
rosewater: quick rosewater
  chocolate mousses 164

S

sage butter 78
salad dressings: herby lemon dressing 48
  lime dressing 106
  my everyday salad dressing 11
salads: bulgur tabbouleh with grilled vegetables 110
  chickpea Greek salad with herby lemon dressing 48
  harvest salad with kale, apple, beetroot & grilled halloumi 76
  kale Caesar salad 85
  Mexican bean salad 106
  salmon niçoise 28
  sunshine salad 107
salmon: potato cakes with smoked salmon 26
  salmon niçoise 28
salsa: fish tacos with salsa & pea guacamole 144
  salsa rustica 82
sea bass: sea bass ceviche with lime, chilli & capers 21
  sea bass & spring onion in a wild garlic broth 141
seafood pot, Montauk 56
shallots, mustard, honey & tarragon chicken traybake with parsnips & 62
Sicilian aubergine stew with cauliflower & almond rice 79
smoked salmon, potato cakes with 26
sorbet, strawberry & elderflower 171
soufflés: cheese soufflé tart with walnut-crusted pastry 140
  foolproof three cheese soufflé 50
soups: chicken noodle soup 37
  French onion soup with Gruyère toasts 47
  green gazpacho 17
  noodle soup with chilli, ginger & green vegetables 122
  sea bass & spring onion in a wild garlic broth 141
  sunshine soup 99
  vegetable wonton & ginger broth 96
spaghetti, ginger & preserved lemon crab 32
Spanish chicken & rice 64
Spanish fish stew 52
spiced chicken & chickpea curry 58
spinach: Bella bean casserole 51
  chicken Florentine 35
  chickpea, spinach & butternut squash stew 119
  coconut & spinach dal 121
  spiced chicken & chickpea curry 58
  spinach, leek & feta filo tart 123
  Thai curry noodles 92
split red lentils: coconut & spinach dal 121

spring green pearl barley risotto 115
spring onions: sea bass & spring onion in a wild garlic broth 141
squash: chickpea, spinach & butternut squash stew 119
  crispy galette with butternut squash, feta & olives 19
  roast butternut squash carbonara 112
  Thai curry noodles 92
squid: slow-cooked squid with olives, tomatoes & garlic 31
steak: steak frites & 10-minute Béarnaise 40
  steak with creamy mushroom linguine 150
stews: chickpea, spinach & butternut squash stew 119
  Sicilian aubergine stew with cauliflower & almond rice 79
  Spanish fish stew 52
storecupboard essentials 8
strawberry & elderflower sorbet 171
sunflower seeds: kale Caesar salad 85
sunshine salad 107
sunshine soup 99
sweet potatoes: aromatic lamb & sweet potato casserole 68
  four ways with baked sweet potatoes & hummus 109
  harvest salad with kale, apple, beetroot & grilled halloumi 76
  sweet potato falafels with harissa dip 81
  sweet potato gnocchi with sage butter 78
  sweet potato wedges 69
sweetcorn: Mexican bean salad 106

T

tabbouleh: bulgur tabbouleh with grilled vegetables 110
tacos: fish tacos with salsa & pea guacamole 144
tagine, chicken 61
tarts: cheese soufflé tart with walnut-crusted pastry 140
  peach tarte tatin with orange blossom cream 167
  spinach, leek & feta filo tart 123
  vegan chocolate tart with hazelnut crust 168
Thai curry noodles 92
three-bean chilli 136–7
tiramisu 162
tofu: Thai curry noodles 92
tomatoes: aromatic lamb & sweet potato casserole 68
  Bella bean casserole 51
  buona amatriciana 41
  chicken tagine 61
  chickpea Greek salad with herby

lemon dressing 48
  chickpea, spinach & butternut squash stew 119
  huevos rancheros 89
  Indian coconut & tomato fish curry 129
  Italian pork & beef ragù 154
  Margherita risotto 118
  ricotta meatballs with polenta 149
  salmon niçoise 28
  slow-cooked squid with olives, tomatoes & garlic 31
  Spanish fish stew 52
  three-bean chilli 136–7
tortillas: fish tacos with salsa & pea guacamole 144
traybakes: Montauk seafood pot 56
  mustard, honey & tarragon chicken traybake with shallots & parsnips 62
tuna, lemon & caper pasta 126

V

vegan chocolate tart with hazelnut crust 168
vegetables: bulgur tabbouleh with grilled vegetables 110
  creamy polenta with green vegetables & gremolata 100
  egg-fried rice with green vegetables 20
  noodle soup with chilli, ginger & green vegetables 122
  Thai curry noodles 92
  vegetable wonton & ginger broth 96
  see also individual types of vegetable

W

walnuts: carrot cake 170
  cheese soufflé tart with walnut-crusted pastry 140
wedges, sweet potato 69
wild garlic: sea bass & spring onion in a wild garlic broth 141
wontons: vegetable wonton & ginger broth 96

Y

yogurt: butter chicken curry 133
  harissa dip 81
  mint & basil yogurt dip 90

UK/US Glossary

Aubergine = eggplant

Bicarbonate of soda = baking soda

Black-eyed beans = black-eyed peas

Caster sugar = superfine sugar

Clingfilm = plastic wrap

Coriander = cilantro

Cornflour = cornstarch

Courgette = zucchini

Double cream = heavy cream

Frying pan = skillet

Gram flour = chickpea flour

Icing sugar = confectioners' sugar

Pepper = bell pepper

Plain flour = all-purpose flour

Self-raising flour = self-rising flour

Single cream = light cream

Spring onions = scallions

Acknowledgements

I want to start by thanking Dora Kazmierak, the photographer for this book. Dora has been a friend of mine for many years and is one of the most talented people I know. She has put endless hours into helping me create this book and my last book, *Clodagh's Suppers*. Such a beautiful person, who I am so lucky to know and get to work with.

Vicky Orchard, the editor. Thank you Vicky for your constant support, ideas and push to make sure this book was made! You have been fabulous to work with.

Lizzie Harris and Hanna Miller, the food stylists and cooks for the book! You are always such a dream to work with and make everything look so beautiful.

Lucy Gowans, the designer. Thank you for all the many variations and for the creative input you made to the book.

Harry Herbert, my darling. Thank you for your constant support and saying that every dish I make is sensational even when it's not. I love you with all my heart.

To my business partner Al Corfield, you have been the rainbow in my life this year.

And to our two doggies, Alfie and Nolly, for the snuggles and constant love.

Love Clo xxx